£1-50

LAKELAND TRAILS

Tony Wimbush

MOUNTAIN DAWN

ISBN Paperback 0 9532483 0 5

While every care has been taken by the author in compiling this book all the routes included are undertaken at the individual's own risk. The inclusion of a route should not be taken as implying a legal right of way or access. If the reader is in doubt the landowner should be consulted. While information in this book was believed to be correct at the time of going to press it is inevitable that addresses and the availability of publications may change. The author cannot accept responsibility for any inconvenience this may cause the reader.

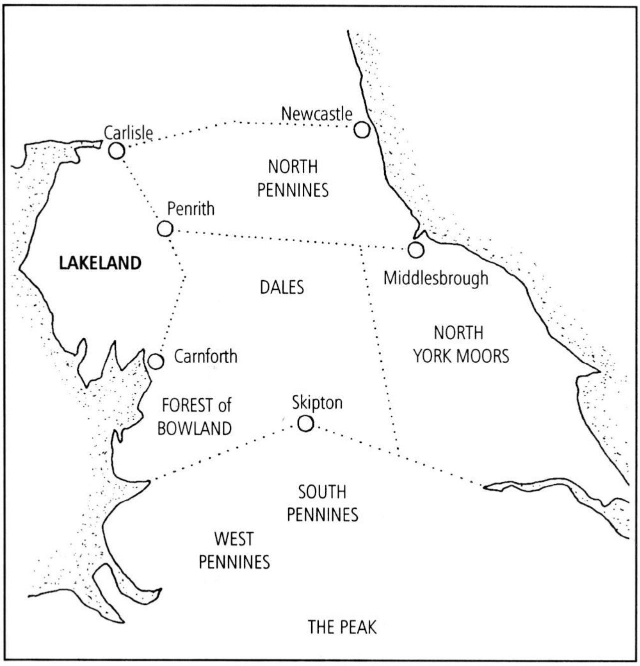

First published in 1998 by
Mountain Dawn Publications
10 Beaufort Grove
Bradford BD2 4L J

British Library Cataloguing-in-Publication Data:
A catalogue record is available for this book from the British Library.

Designed by Tony Wimbush

Printed and bound by
Smith Settle
Ilkley Road
Otley
West Yorkshire
LS21 3JP

Cover: Top - towards Langdale, bottom - Wasdale

CONTENTS

Acknowledgements 4
Preface and Introductory Notes 5

Heritage Trails 7
Lakeland Heritage Trail 10
Mountain Heritage Trail 18

Trail Guide 23
Allerdale Ramble 27
Back O' Skidda 28
Charnley Way 29
Cistercian Way 30
Cumberland Way 31
Cumbria Coastal Way 32
Cumbria Way 33
Duddon Horseshoe 34
Duddon Landscape 35
Duddon Triangle 36
Everest Challenge 37
Furness Boundary Walk 38
Furness Five Trigs 39
Furness Way 40
Grasmere Skyline 41
Haematite Trail 42
High Street Stroll 47
Kirkbymoor Round 48
Lake District Boundary Walk 49
Lakeland Ridges Challenge 50
Lakeland Round 51
Rydal Round 52
Thirlmere Round 53
Traditional Hostels Lakes Walk 54
Wainwright's Lake District Tour 55
Walk Round The Lakes 56
West Lakes Way 57
Westmorland Heritage Walk 58
Westmorland Way 59
Whicham Valley Five Trigs 60
More Lakeland Trails 61
Shorter Lakeland Trails 64
Lakeland Links 65

Peaks Lakes and Rounds 67
Bob Graham Round 68
The Wainwrights 70
The Lakes Two-thousands 73
Mountain Challenges 74
Horseshoes and Rounds 76

Information 79
Information Centres 80
Accommodation 81
Transport 83
Organisations 84
General 85

Christian Aid 86
Amnesty International 87

Index 88

CONTENTS

Acknowledgements & Sources

Quotations

Page 5 A Westmorland Legend taken from Lakeland Today, Arthur Knowles, Lakeland Publishing Co. Ltd., 1983
Page 9 A H Griffin, Freeman of the Hills, Robert Hale Ltd, 1978
Page 27 & 31 F Singleton, The English Lakes, B T Batsford, 1954
Page 32 E Waugh, taken from Over Sands to the Lakes, exact date not known - 19th century
Page 33 Ruth McKenny, taken from F. Singleton's The English Lakes, B T Batsford, 1954
Page 36, 38 & 42 J Lofthouse, The Curious Traveller Lancaster to Lakeland, Robert Hale Limited, 1956
Page 37 Archbishop Tutu, taken from the Christian Aid leaflet Changing the Rules, 1996
Page 40 W Heaton Cooper, The Lakes, Frank Peters Publishing, 1966
Page 43 H Brown, Hamish's Mountain Walk, Granada Publishing Ltd, Paladin Books, 1980
Page 43 M Cudahy, Wild Trails to Far Horizons, Unwin Hyman, 1989
Page 43 W T Palmer, In Lakeland Dells and Fells, Chatto & Windus, 1903
Page 44 M Marples, Shanks's Pony, The Country Book Club, 1959
Page 44 A Knowles, Lakeland Today, The Lakeland Publishing Co. Ltd,1983
Page 44 N Nicholson, The Lakers, Robert Hale & Company, 1955
Page 45 H Davies, Wainwright the Biography, Michael Joseph, 1995
Page 45 A Wainwright, A Coast to Coast Walk, Westmorland Gazette, 1973. Now published by Michael Joseph
Page 46 M MacBride, Wild Lakeland, A&C Black Ltd, 1922
Page 46 P Withers, In a Cumberland Dale, Jonathan Cape, 1940
Page 47 H H Symonds, Walking in the Lake District, Alexander Maclehose & Co.,1933
Page 49 G K Dugdale, The Lake District Boundary Walk, Westmorland Gazette, 1996
Page 51 T Lawton, Tom Lawton's Lakeland Round, Ward Locke, 1995
Page 52 J Payne, taken from Lakeland Today, Arthur Knowles, Lakeland Publishing Co. Ltd., 1983
Page 53 E M Ward, Days in Lakeland, Methuen, 1929
Page 54 F S Smythe, The Spirit of the Hills, Hodder & Stoughton Ltd., 1935
Page 58 M Creighton, The Story of Some English Shires, The Religious Tract society, 1897
Page 59 M J B Baddeley, The English Lake District, Ward, Lock & Co., Limited, date not known
Page 65 St Augustine, The Confessions, 4th Century
Page 70 A Wainwright, The Western Fells, Westmorland Gazette, 1965 now published by Michael Joseph
Page 73 E Moss, All Those Two-thousands, Rucksack Club Journal, 1952 reproduced with their permission

Technical Support

R M Wimbush - technical computer support, scanning, printing camera-ready copy
B Tristram - data transfer

Information on routes

Brian Richmond for permission to reproduce details of the Duddon Horseshoe, Duddon Triangle, Furness Five Trigs, Grasmere Skyline, Thirlmere Round and Whicham Valley Five Trigs.
Joyce Sidebottom - Back O'Skidda and High Street Stroll
Jim Strother - Rydal Round
Graham Dugdale - Lake District Boundary Walk
Monica Shone - Joss Naylor's Lakeland Challenge
Carol Campbell - Furness Boundary Walk
Kate Clarkson - Duddon Landscape Walk
Oxfam Campaigns office - Everest Challenge
All authors and publications listed in the Trail Guide

General Information

Ken Smith, Smith Settle
Ulverston, Whitehaven, Cockermouth and Keswick Tourist Information Centres
Eskdale Youth Hostel
Brian Smith, LDWA Path information
LDWA Handbook and Strider magazines
Fell Runners' Association magazines
Charlotte Prager, Ramblers' Association
Mike Cudahy, Rucksack Club
Amnesty International
Christian Aid
Fred Rogerson, Chairman of the Bob Graham Club.
Alan Castle, Hillwalkers' Register
Studmarks on the Summits, Bill Smith - information on mountain challenges and classic rounds
Trans-Pennine Publishing information on the Shap Stroll
The Rocks and Landscape of the Keswick Area, Dr Alan Smith, Cumbria RISG Group
Thirlmere Way, Tim Capelli, Sigma Leisure, 1992

Lake Heritage Routes

Checking route descriptions: J Wimbush, J Nicholson, M Chorney, J Newmark, M Scott

Proof reading

J Wimbush, J Nicholson, J Palmer, S Palmer

> In the time of middle earth, timeless aeons before the fall from grace, there was a place where man could pass quite freely between earth and paradise. So that men's minds should not be dazed by the shocking beauty of paradise, the place was made in the celestial image, a high place of ethereal beauty, masked in soft mist, earthly yet shot through with a spirit beyond the range of men's minds. So perfect it could be none other than the roots of heaven.
>
> A Westmorland legend

The Lake District is to many people a heaven on earth, a retreat from the turmoil of the world and all its affairs, a place where the peace and harmony of the natural world still prevails. For those of us who already know the Lakeland fells, thoughts of them will stir up our own personal memories and impressions. We will be reminded that some of the best moments in our lives have been spent among them whether it be with family, friends or simply alone on their heights. Such is the power and influence of the fells. Yet all this can be produced by a few earthly elements. The Lake District is not even, by world-wide standards, a place of spectacular dimensions. But that is, perhaps, its appeal. It is surely a constant wonder that such basic elements as rock, grass, sky and water can combine with the changing seasons or the hour of the day to produce such extraordinary variety, such subtle charm and such infinite beauty that, once experienced, it has the power to continually draw and inspire us in so many different ways.

It has to be said that the only way to fully appreciate the Lakes is on foot. People walk for different reasons. Some measure a walk by the miles covered or the number of peaks ascended, others by places visited or things seen or studied, while for others a walk simply provides a rhythm and a reason for relaxation or pondering great thoughts. It is amazing that the simple act of putting one foot in front of the other can be a source of enjoyment in so many different ways. From an evening stroll by a lakeside to an arduous mountain challenge, few landscapes can give so much pleasure to so many people. Walking is all things to all people. Long may it remain so.

There is only one thing better than a day in the Lake District and that is two days or even longer. This is really the purpose of this book, to encourage more people to leave their cars behind and discover the unique and simple pleasure of a continuous walk, finding a different resting place each night; to experience the satisfaction in the purpose and discipline of reaching their destination by traversing the landscape under their own steam in their own time. This book is packed with information on how to do just that. It is full of good things and good ideas. Most of them are by other people and I would readily acknowledge my debt to their authors. My main purpose has been to bring their walks to a wider audience, especially routes which are only published locally or privately or support some charity and are not available from national booksellers. A stroll has also been taken round a small library of literature on the Lake District, walking and mountains. This has been used to add some light and colour to what might otherwise have been a dull scene of facts, figures and maps. Much has been written on the Lakes; it has inspired whole shelves of superlatives from the mystery and pantheism of Wordsworth to the love and affection of Wainwright. But let the hills speak for themselves. They speak of simple truth and simple beauty. They teach contentment, goodwill and wisdom. Yes, they even speak of the boundaries of heaven itself. Listen and you will hear. Listen. Listen carefully.

Tony Wimbush

INTRODUCTORY NOTES

The purpose of this book

- ☐ Introducing novices or casual walkers to the pleasures of trail walking along an easy route that can be readily completed in sections - **The Lakeland Heritage Trail.** This is intended to help more people discover the satisfaction of linking together the network of Lakeland paths into continuous routes, or trails, that can involve up to several days walking whether for a weekend, a week or a fortnight.

- ☐ Offering first time visitors, particularly those from overseas, two trails that can be readily completed in a weekend or so yet give a satisfying introduction to the unique charm and character of the region - **The Lakeland Heritage Trail** or **The Lakeland Heritage Mountain Trail .**

- ☐ Encouraging more people to leave their cars behind to avoid the congestion of roads and car parks and use what were the old ways of exploring the Lake District - walking tours and public transport.

- ☐ Providing a **Trail Guide** as a summary of published routes to give visitors an easy and convenient way of choosing which routes might be suitable and of interest. This is also intended to help promote some of the lesser known trails which are only published locally or privately and are not widely available.

- ☐ Offering experienced walkers and fell runners, who want to test their fitness and stamina, a series of one day challenges, courtesy of Brian Richmond, together with a brief survey of the established mountain challenges on offer in the Lakes - **Peaks, Lakes and Rounds**.

- ☐ Providing sources of **Information** on accommodation, public transport, walking and local conservation.

Notes for overseas or first time visitors

None of the routes in the national park have any official waymarking although public footpaths are often signposted from roads; gates and stiles may also be marked. On the hills (fells) footpaths are often confirmed by piles of stones (cairns). There are no painted markers common on European trails. Some fells can have a network of cairned paths particularly on the summits. As this can be confusing in mist, it is important to check the direction being followed using a compass.

Choice of routes - most walkers have their own preferences when it comes to selecting routes but those unfamiliar with the area may appreciate some guidance. Consider starting with one of the following for a combination of easy access to the start point, a reasonable range of accommodation and a good guidebook with wet weather options.

Easy to moderate valley and pass routes
Lakeland Heritage Trail - 17 mls up to 2-3 days
Traditional Hostels Walk - 65 mls up to 5-6 days
Furness Way - 75 mls up to 5-6 days

Strenuous high-level routes
Lakeland Heritage Mountain Trail - 25 mls up to 2-3 days
Everest Challenge - 83 mls up to 6-7 days
Walk Round The Lakes - 145 mls up to 15 days

A Short Anthology

Scattered across the pages that follow are words from a wide range of twentieth century writers, most of which are regrettably no longer in print, although much of what they have to say is surprisingly refreshing. In a way this has created a short anthology from the rich library of literature that both the Lakes and walking have inspired. Anyone with a particular interest in this can obtain copies from libraries or second-hand book shops. Titles and publishers are listed on page 4 under acknowledgements and sources.

A Guide To Walking

THE LAKELAND HERITAGE TRAIL & THE LAKELAND HERITAGE MOUNTAIN TRAIL

LAKELAND HERITAGE

HERITAGE TRAILS

THE LAKELAND HERITAGE TRAIL

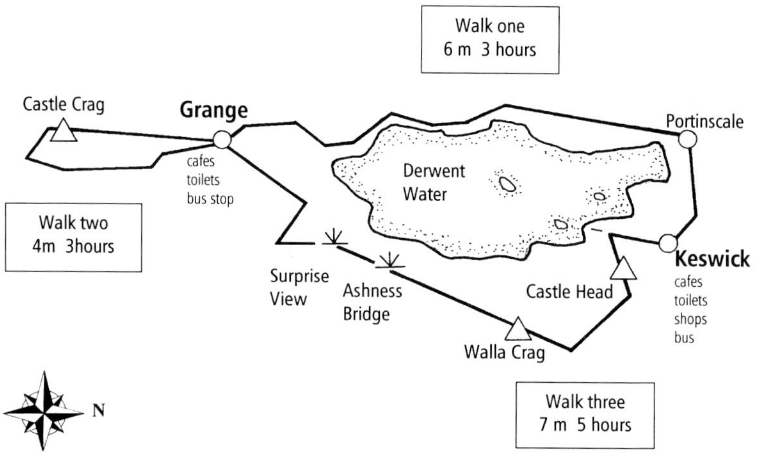

THE LAKELAND HERITAGE MOUNTAIN TRAIL

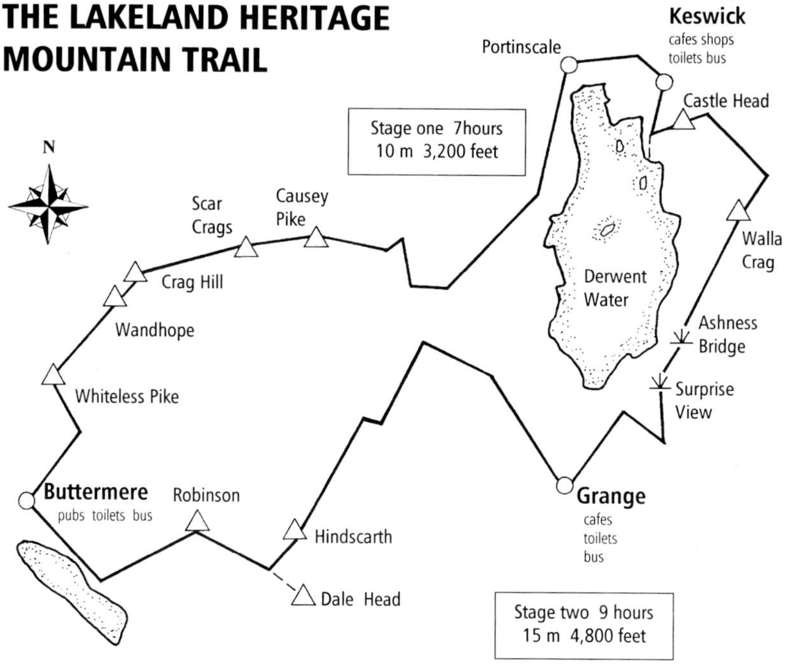

Suddenly you realise how fortunate you are - to be active and healthy, far from motorcars and television and strikes and violence, high up on a Lakeland mountain in sunshine, rain, cloud, wind or snow. Everyday throughout the seasons the hills are different, every day you can find something new. Surely it is all a matchless heritage to be guarded with constant devotion and common sense. Whatever happens, the hills will always be there and, in time, if we approach the heights with humility, respect and experience, we can win the freedom of the most wonderful mountain country in England.

A H Griffin, 1978

Some might say that the rich and diverse heritage of the Lakes could not be exhausted in a whole lifetime's exploration let alone encompassed in a couple of trails which take up a long weekend. And they would probably be right. However, these two mini tours provide ample opportunity to absorb those special elements which allow the Lake District to occupy such a unique place in the heritage of Britain if not the world.

These trails have been devised with two types of visitor in mind. Firstly those who make regular visits and require a route that can be completed in an extended weekend or less. Secondly those who do not know the Lakes, such as overseas visitors, and wish to explore a small area well. Both routes start and finish at Keswick and have been specifically designed to be car-free. The most rewarding way to complete both of the trails is by walking on consecutive days staying overnight at either Grange on the Lakeland Trail or Buttermere for the Mountain Trail. Alternatively Keswick could be used as a convenient base and public transport used to return there each day.

At the other extreme both routes will provide a worthy challenge to fell runners and others with a healthy streak of insanity who wish to do a non-stop round!

The English Lakes North West OS Outdoor Leisure Map is recommended for both walks.

Lakeland Heritage Trail - 17 miles

walk one Keswick to Grange - 6 miles
walk two Grange Circular - 4 miles
walk three Grange to Keswick - 7 miles

This route has been designed as an introduction to long distance walking specifically with the novice and casual walker in mind. Each day becomes slightly more strenuous. Day one is flat, day two is shorter but includes the ascent of one of the most delightful fells in the Lakes while day three combines both more ascent and distance. None of the walks takes more than a few hours so there is ample time to rest or pursue any particular outdoor interests.

Mountain Trail - 25 miles and 8,000 feet

Stage one Keswick to Buttermere
10 miles and 3,200 feet of climbing

Stage two Buttermere to Keswick
15 miles and 4,800 feet of climbing

This route has been devised with the seasoned walker in mind who perhaps likes an element of challenge. With 8,000 feet of ascent in its 25 mile journey this represents a relatively tough route. Unless the weather forecast is favourable the less demanding Lakeland Trail should be considered.

The first stage can be comfortably completed in a day. The second stage is a long day but can be made easier by an overnight stop at Grange. This would then allow a leisurely trip back to Keswick on the third day with time to spend there or make the journey home.

Accommodation ....see page 82
Public Transport ....see page 83
Badges & Certificates......see page 22
Bad weather options......see page 22
Safety and Equipment....see page 85

LAKELAND HERITAGE TRAIL

Keswick to Grange

6 miles
walk one

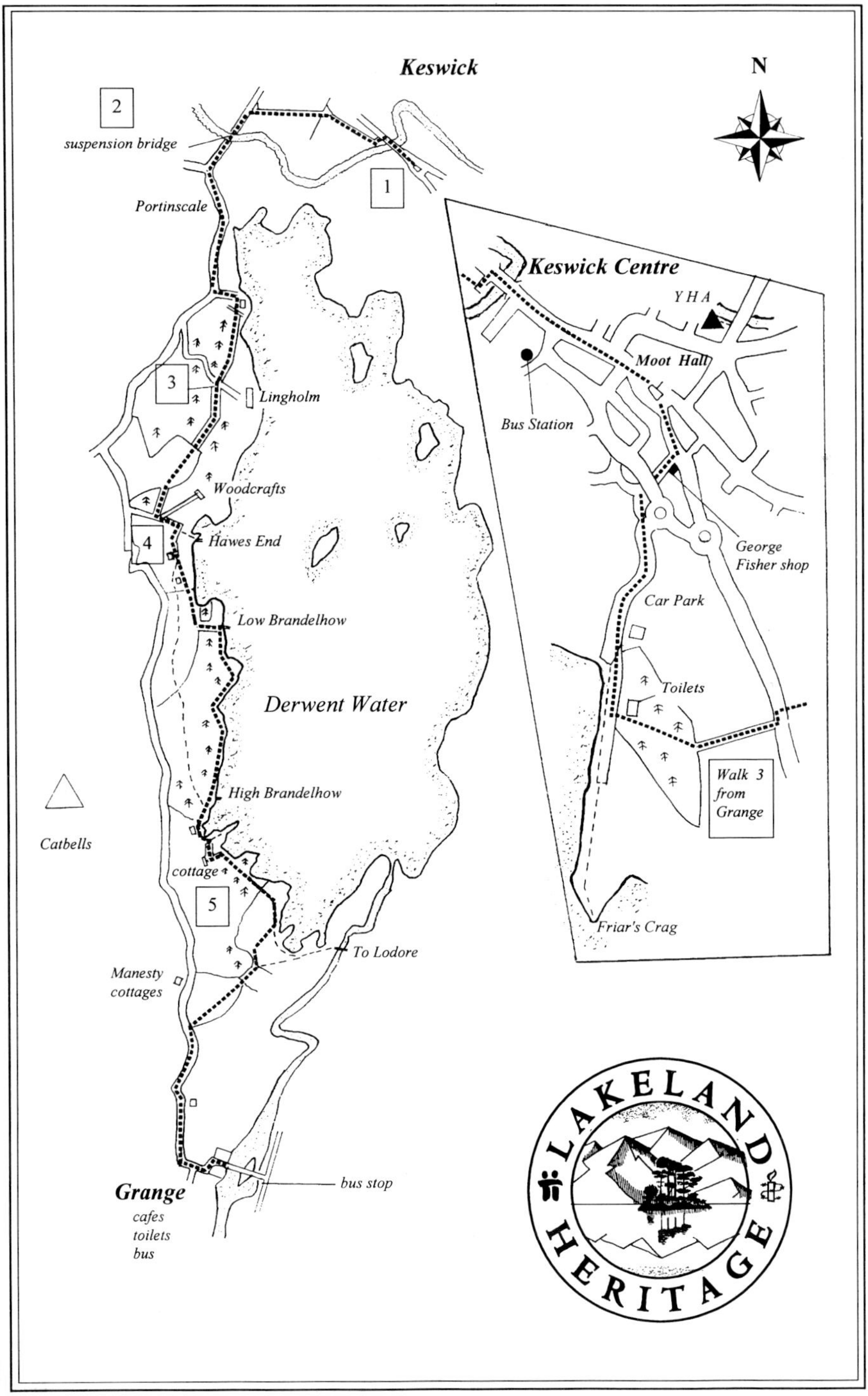

LAKELAND HERITAGE TRAIL

Keswick to Grange

Allow 3 hours

The first section of the Heritage Trail leads quickly away from the pleasant surrounds of Keswick to join the Cumbrian Way as it follows gentle wooded paths along the west side of Derwent Water.

1 From the Moot Hall Tourist Information Centre turn down Main Street to pass the Skiddaw Hotel on left. Continue straight on through main shopping area to reach bridge over the River Greta. Cross and immediately turn left sp (signpost) **Portinscale**. Soon turn right through gate sp **Public Footpath Portinscale**. Continue on clear path by hedge across field to metal gate and across second field to reach two gates and a tarmac lane. Turn left and cross suspension bridge.

2 Continue along lane to bear left past Derwentwater Hotel. Turn left at junction in 400 yards, pass Derwent Bank and shortly turn left sp **Public Road to Lake & Nichol End** down broad track. At the boat landings bear right round back of marine shop to ascend track which shortly emerges by house. Cross drive (to Fawe Park) to track opposite sp **Footpath** and follow through woods to emerge at the entrance to Lingholm Gardens.

3 Take the gate on the right of the entrance, sign **public footpath to Catbells**, and follow a fenced path to a wooden gate into a field (Catbells is straight in front, Rowlings End and Causey Pike are to the right). Cross to reach small gate/bridge then ascend on fenced path to reach tarmac lane at gate.

Mountain Trail walkers should leave the route here **- see page 19**

4 Turn left sp **The Lake - MANESTY** and pass entrance to Derwent Bay Woodcrafts (worth a visit but watch out for bears!) in the direction of Hawse End Centre. Pass sp **Lake shore path** (launch jetty points left), and shortly turn left at Hawse End sign (marker- left) along tarmac lane to sp **Lakeside Path - MANESTY**. Turn left through metal kissing gate and follow track to gateway and kissing gate. Continue on to bear left between fences to gate and cross field to landing stage at Low Brandelhow. Pass through gate and follow lakeside path for nearly a mile to High Brandelhow boat landing. Continue by edge of lake on pebbled beach to climb wooden stile. Continue straight on to reach track and bear left, cross stream and pass white house to right (Brandelhow). Pass through gate (sign footpath only), shortly turn right at junction and follow broad track to cottage.

5 Turn left at small sp **FOOTPATH TO LODORE.** Follow path by fence, along lakeside and through woods to find gate in wall (30 yards to right of stile by lake). Continue ahead soon to join boarded path over marshy ground. Gradually bear right over more boards and continue on path to another set of boards. Do not cross but turn right on path across open ground towards wall and wood, bear left through gate onto good track. Soon go through second gate and follow clear track to meet road at sp **Public Footpath to Lodore.** Turn left to reach Grange within fifteen minutes.

- ☐ Cross bridge for bus back to Keswick.
- ☐ Toilets and cafes in village.

LAKELAND HERITAGE TRAIL

Grange to Castle Crag and return

4 miles
walk two

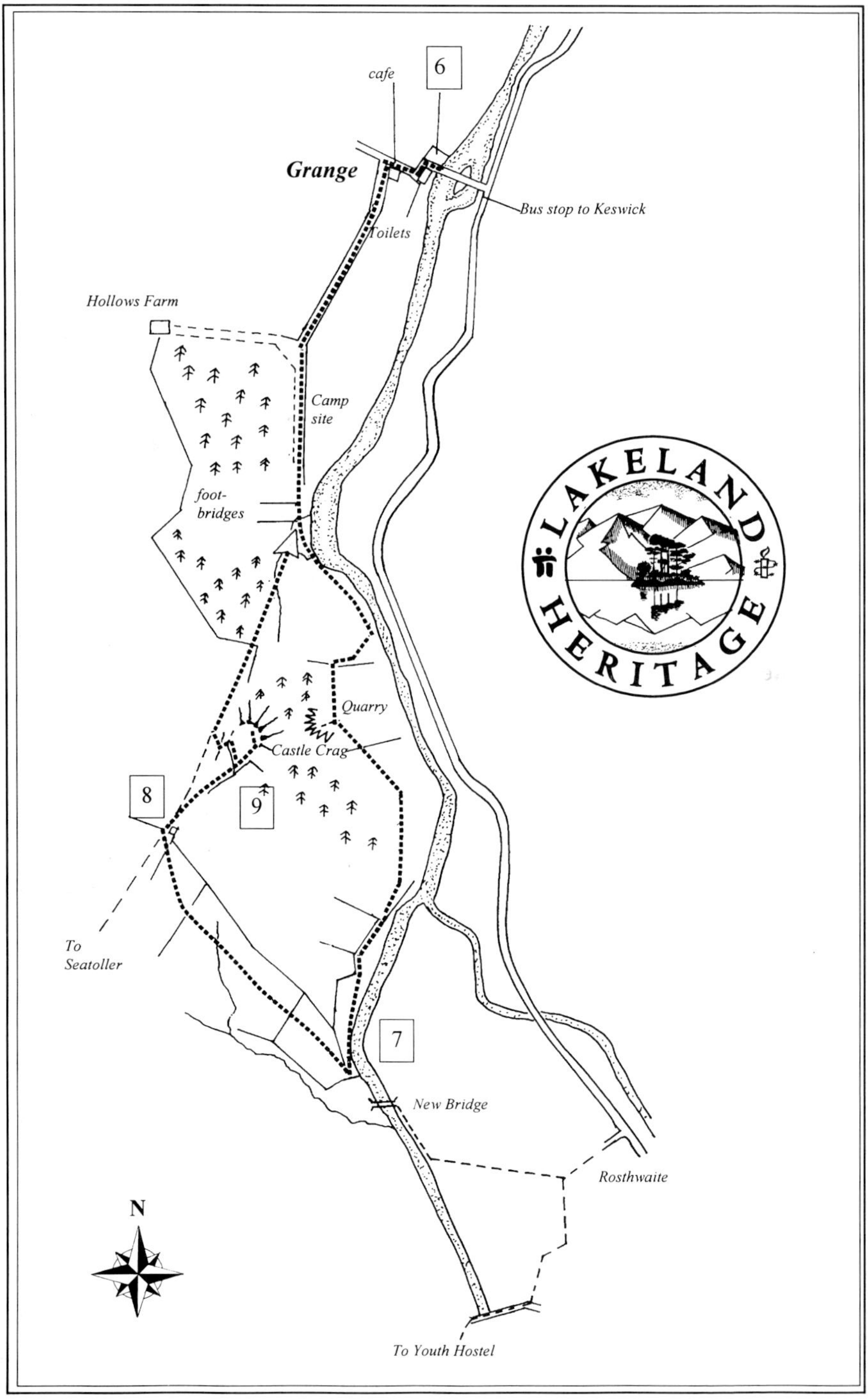

LAKELAND HERITAGE TRAIL

Grange to Castle Crag and return

Allow 3 hours

An enchanting stretch of path by the crystal-clear waters of the River Derwent is contrasted with a climb to the top of one of the most memorable little fells in the Lakes. The final steep stony climb to the summit yields an aerial view of the valley as it reaches out towards Derwent Water and the majestic Skiddaw.

6 From the village side of the bridge continue along the road a short way to turn left by Grange cafe along a tarmaced bridleway sp (signpost) **Honister, Rosthwaite, Seatoller**. Within 500 yards (at camping signs) turn left on rough track passing campsite. When wall on left ends continue straight on to join riverside path. Soon bear right to cross footbridge and continue along riverside to another footbridge on right to find sp **Footpath Rosthwaite** (you will return later to this point after completing the circuit to Castle Crag). Continue straight on to pass through gate and continue along firm track. This soon turns away from the river, flat at first then ascending, to meet a wall on the left. Keep ascending with wall to left to pass through wall opening on stony path. Continue until fork in the path to turn left down hill following cairned path which passes through wall opening. Follow until path eventually draws closer to the river with fence nearby. Continue with fence on left and shortly pass through gate, then with fence then wall on right eventually join riverbank. Continue by river and shortly pass through gate and immediately turn right to enter adjacent gate.

7 Take vague path ascending field to stile. Continue to ascend on clear path to cross stream and broken wall (view back down valley). Here the path bears right and when the wall comes into view bear right to the field corner and go through wooden gate.

8 Continue straight ahead to join broad track and turn right. As track begins to descend (viewpoint of Derwentwater and Skiddaw with Castle Crag on near right) look for vague path ascending on right. Follow to fence, ignore first stile in fence and continue to a second stile near wall. Cross and then take ladder stile over wall (you will return to near this point after ascending Castle Crag). Bear right to ascend the steep winding slopes of Castle Crag to reach the summit.

9 Descend retracing your steps to the wall but ignore ladder stiles and bear right to follow wall/fence. Find stile and ladder then descend on winding track to reach stile in wall. Descend to join broad track at large cairn. Turn right and gradually descend to wooden gate. Continue descent, cross stream by wooden footbridge and follow track to river at sp which you left earlier. Cross wooden footbridge and follow riverside path to join good track back to Grange.

☐ Cross bridge for bus back to Keswick
☐ Toilets and cafes in village

LAKELAND HERITAGE TRAIL

Grange to Keswick

7 miles
walk three

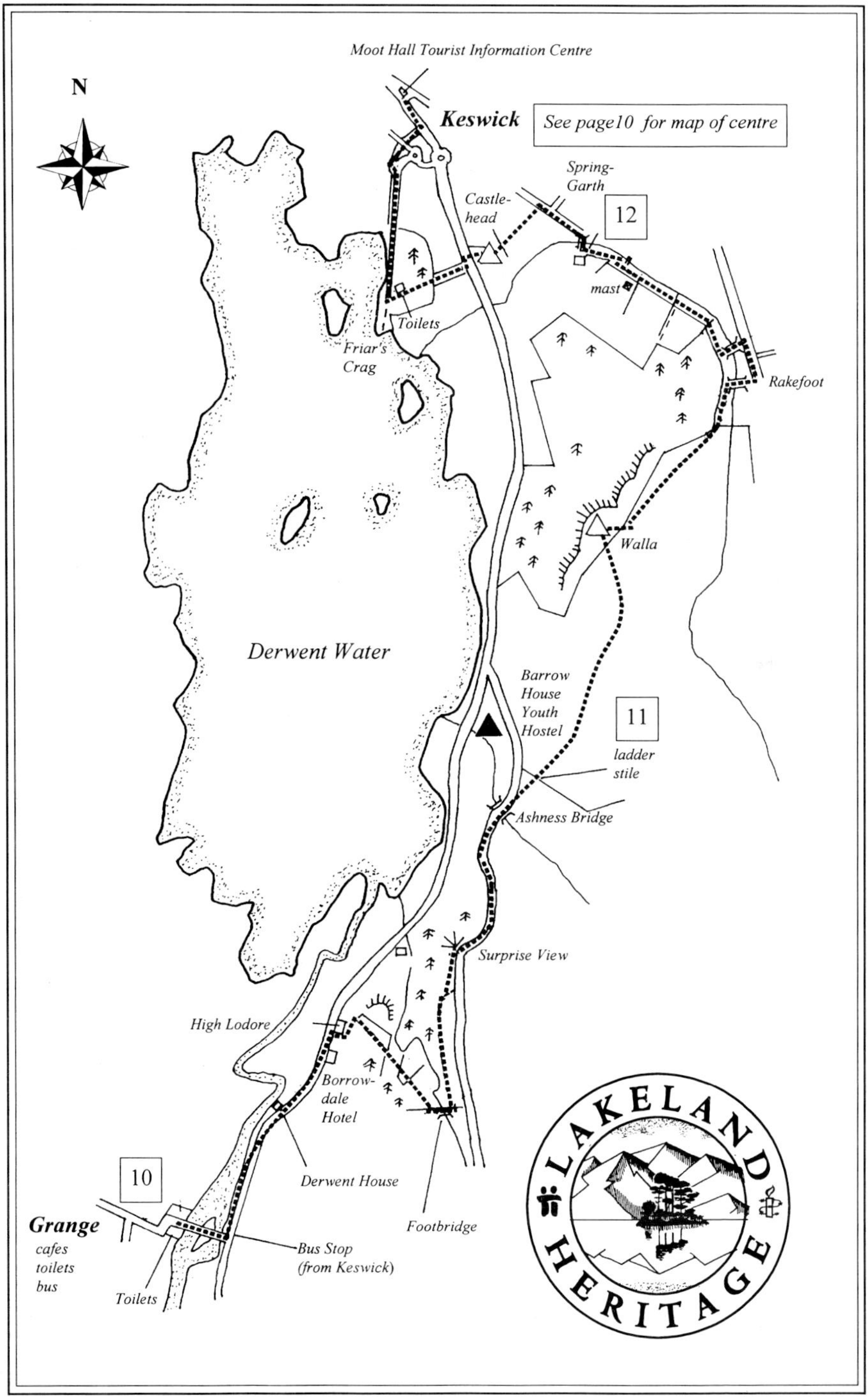

LAKELAND HERITAGE TRAIL

Grange to Keswick

Allow 4 hours

The delights of Borrowdale are left behind to take in some of Lakeland's best known panoramas including Surprise View, Ashness Bridge and Walla Crag. Castlehead provides a final opportunity to gaze upon Derwent Water and its sublime mountain backcloth before returning to the friendly bustle of Keswick.

10 After crossing the bridge from Grange village turn left and join riverside path. Where road turns right leave river to rejoin road and follow past **Derwent House**. Continue on to pass **Borrowdale Hotel** on right then shortly take track sp (signpost) **public footpath** just before High Lodore Farm (seasonal refreshments). Bear left round back of farm ascending steeply. Shortly track forks, bear right and ascend steeply on winding track for 15 minutes to reach a broken wall. Continue straight ahead descending initially to cross stream. Continue on to wooden gate over-looking waterfall and follow fence to stile. Climb and ascend on rocky path until it levels and reaches wooden gate. Pass through gate and bear left over bridge and continue by wall shortly to pass through gate. Continue on broad path bearing right to ascend gradually through the woods. About 20 yards before road bear left to stay in wood on undulating path which meanders parallel to the road to emerge at Surprise View overlooking Derwent Water. Turn left down road to reach Ashness Bridge. Cross and immediately take path on right sp **Great Wood and Keswick**.

11 Ascend to ladder stile and continue, bearing right ascending on obvious path for one long mile to reach wall and stile. Cross and shortly reach summit cairn. From summit bear right to wall and stile, climb and turn left to descend by wall to eventually bear left to stile and gate at **National Trust** sign. Continue descent and cross footbridge at Rakefoot. Turn left onto tarmac lane. Within 200 yards look for hidden gate on left sp **Keswick and Great Wood**. Cross bridge and turn right to descend by stream. Continue through wooden gates ignoring footpath on left to Great Wood and Borrowdale. Continue down past mast to sharp right bend after which turn left to descend by stream to gate. Continue straight through farm and bear right over bridge.

12 Continue down tarmac lane to pass **Spring Garth** road on right and within 100 yards take narrow path on left sp **Castlehead and Lake Road**. Shortly pass through wooden gate and ascend Castlehead. From viewpoint retrace steps back to fence corner. Turn left past wooden seat and reach road (care!) at **National Trust sign**. Cross road and turn left and shortly turn right sp **To the Lake** along narrow path. At end continue straight on to emerge at boat landings near toilets. Turn right on lakeside path to pass car park. Stay on lefthandside path to pass through subway. Shortly turn right up **Lake Road** (National Park shop on right). Turn left at George Fisher's shop to reach the Moot Hall.

Derwent Water and Beatrix Potter
The Potter family are known to have taken their summer holidays at Lingholm and Fawe Park on the west side of the lake between 1885 and 1907. Much of this area provided the backcloth and inspiration for Beatrix Potter's illustrations and characters.

St Herbert's Isle, Derwent Water
This island in almost the centre of Derwent Water is named after the hermit who made his home there and died in 687 AD. He is associated with St Cuthbert who became prior of Holy Island in 661 AD and was a famous ascetic of the Celtic Church .

Bob Graham
Bob Graham was one of the proprietors of Barrow House which is now Derwent Water Youth Hostel. He set a new Lakeland fell running record in 1932 and has since had a club named after him - see page 68. Fred Rogerson who helped found the Club built a memorial cairn at the back of the hostel a short way from Ashness Bridge. A plaque reads:

In memory of Robert Graham 1889-1966 of Keswick who on 13-14 June 1932 traversed 42 peaks within 24 hours. A record which stood for 28 years.

Keswick
Before its growth as a tourist centre in the eighteenth century Keswick owed much to the mining industry whose remnants are now scattered around the surrounding fells. During the sixteenth century the Keswick area was invaded by hundreds of German miners, some of whom married into local families.
The nearby parish church of Crosthwaite is one of the most interesting in the Lakes. It dates from the twelfth century and is dedicated to St Kentigern. Canon Rawnsley, who helped found the National Trust, was vicar of the parish for 43 years.

National Trust Centenary Sculpture
This is located in Calf Close Bay at grid reference 267 215 and commemorates their centenary year of 1995. It has been created from a boulder of lava brought from the Borrowdale valley. Peter Randell-Page the sculptor has incorporated it into the landscape by taking a local boulder, splitting it and carving ten rings and ten segments to symbolise one hundred years.

Surprise View
This spectacular roadside viewpoint stands some 300 feet above Derwent Water. It is on the rim of the valley created by ice action and overlooks a classic birds foot delta.

Castle Crag and Castlehead
Both these viewpoints are the result of volcanic intrusions which were more resistant to erosion by ice than the surrounding rocks. Castle Crag at under 1000 feet high is the lowest, as well as one of the most memorable, of the Wainwright tops - see page 70.

Grange in Borrowdale
In 1209 the Cistercian monks of Furness Abbey bought the Borrowdale valley as a sheep farm and had a grange at this hamlet. The twin-arched bridge is a favourite among photographers; its picture regularly appears in Lakeland calendars.

Ashness Bridge
This provides the ubiquitous picture postcard view with the noble massif of Skiddaw in the background guarding over Keswick. Its popularity is well deserved.

Walla Crag 1234'
This is another exceptional view-point, if its not raining, achieved with relatively little effort. The distinctive summits of Cat Bells, Causey Pike and Grisedale Pike can be seen while further left is Bassenthwaite Lake and Skiddaw.

Causey Pike 2090'
The distinctive pyramid shape can be readily recognised from all directions but is probably best known as part of the towering backcloth to the town of Keswick. The route from here to Crag Hill is one of Lakeland's finest ridge walks as it makes its way along a lofty promenade between Rigg beck and the Coledale valley.

Crag Hill 2753'
This is the highest point on the mountain trail and the central hub of the Derwent Fells. The flat top, crowned by an O.S. triangulation pillar, provides a superb panorama of northern Lakeland.

Buttermere valley
Every Lakeland valley has its own character and Buttermere displays a scene of infinite mountain grandeur. Its steep-sided flanks come tumbling down from its rocky rim while the head of the valley is dominated by the lofty Fleetwith Pike.
The house at Hassness was originally built by General Benson during the 1800's but was demolished and rebuilt in the 1920's. Today it is a holiday centre run by the Ramblers' Association. Before reaching the house the trail passes through a short tunnel in the rock. This is believed to have been made by the General to keep his men employed in the winter months.
The simple church in Buttermere contains a memorial to Alfred Wainwright.

Haystacks 1958'
Looking across Buttermere from Hassness is the mountain of Haystacks. There on 22 March 1991 the ashes of Alfred Wainwright were scattered by Betty Wainwright on a private visit some two months after his death at eighty-four. As long ago as 1966 he had written ' All I ask for , at the end, is a last resting place by the side of Innominate Tarn, on Haystacks where the water gently laps the gravelly shore and the heather blooms and Pillar and Gable keep unfailing watch'. And so it was.

Hindscarth 2385'
Its finest feature is undoubtedly the ridge walk towards Scope End. The winding track through the heather is a delight to be savoured. After the descent and the crossing of Newlands Beck do not forget to keep looking back as you make your way along the track - Robinson, Hindscarth and Scope End make a perfect photograph.

Newlands valley
Historically the valley was best known as a mining area after several hundred German miners were imported during the sixteenth century. Goldscope mine below what is now called Scope End was the first to be opened. The word derives from Gottes-gaab, "the gift of God", although the miners were hoping to find gold rather than copper.
In contrast it is, today, better known for its hamlet of Little Town and its associations with Beatrix Potter's Mrs Tiggywinkle.

Buttermere

MOUNTAIN TRAIL

Keswick to Buttermere

10 miles
stage one

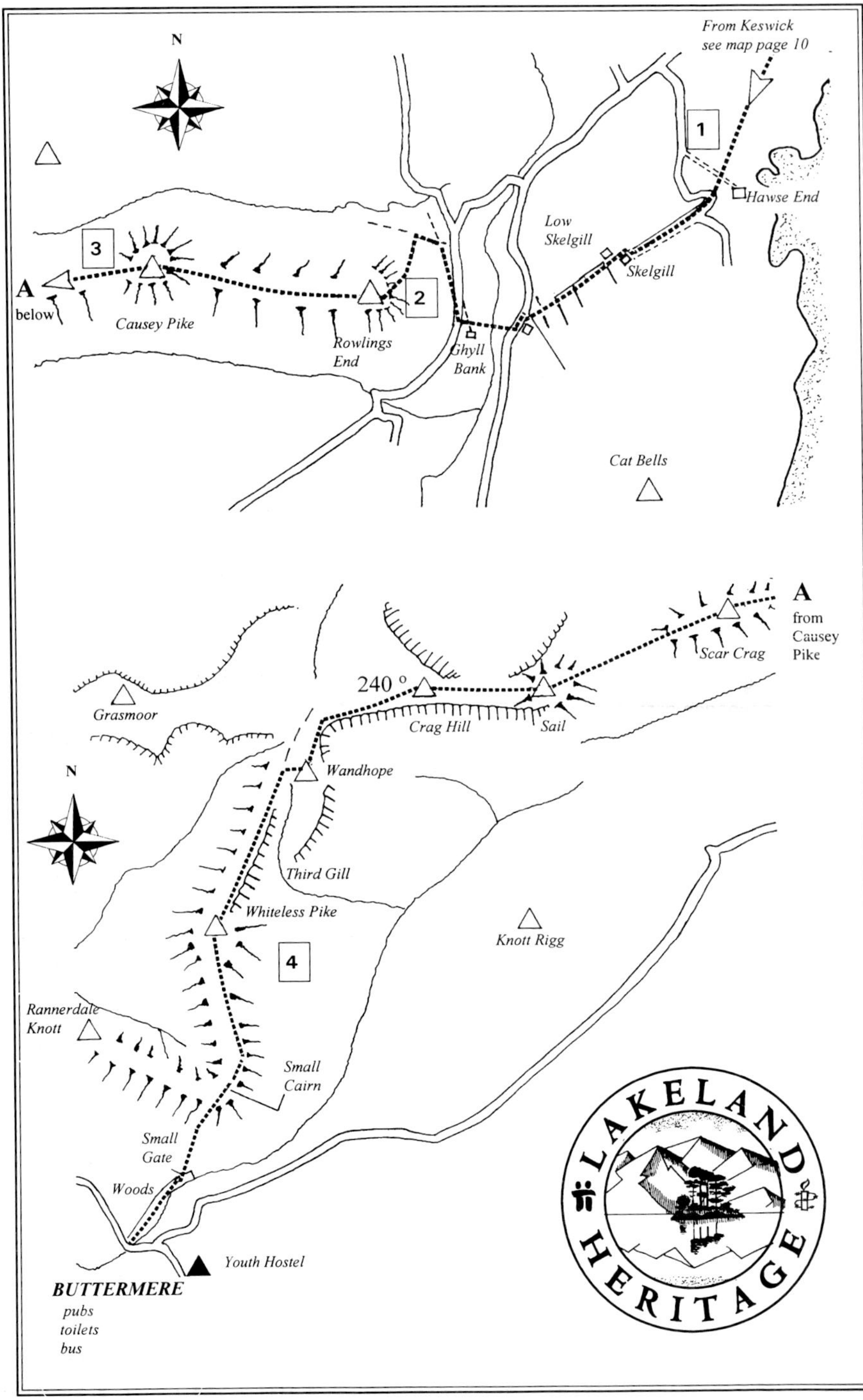

MOUNTAIN TRAIL

Keswick to Buttermere

Allow 7 hours

Man, or woman, and mountain soon meet on this trek across the roof of the Derwent Fells. From these lofty heights waves of hills and ridges lap your feet from every direction. A memorable descent into the majestic Buttermere valley completes the day's outing.

1 The first part of this walk follows the route description of the Heritage Trail as far as the tarmac lane before turning left to Hawse End Centre - see page 11 end of section 3 . Cross the tarmac lane sp (signpost) **Public Footpath CATBELLS** and ascend on good track by wall to join road bend by **National Trust** sign. Continue uphill to cross the cattle grid and leave the road at the next bend along tarmac lane to Skelgill Farm. The pyramid summit of Causey Pike will be on your right if clear. Go through wooden gate, bear right then turn left through wooden gate to Low Skelgill. Pass farmhouse on right and continue straight on to climb stile at wooden gate. Bear right by fence to follow track to second wooden gate and stile. Continue with fence on right to reach third stile and gate. View of Robinson, Hindscarth and Scope End. Climb and cross open field to stile by gate in fence. Cross short boggy section and open field to gate and sp **Public Footpath Skelghyll** at road. Turn left down road and within 40 yards turn right through gate at sp **Public Footpath.** Descend across boggy field to cross wooden bridge. Ascend to right of white house ahead to locate wooden gate. Cross drive and continue to ascend on path to emerge at road at wooden gate **Public Footpath Ghyll Bank**. Turn right for about 60 yards to take path on left sp **Public Footpath.** Follow the path as it contours round the hillside for about 400 yards to a path junction.

2 Here the path meets a stony path which ascends from near a road junction below. Do not continue on the grassy path but bear left uphill on narrow stony path which turns up the valley. In about 120 yards look for steep zig-zag path which ascends to left as the main path starts to level. Take this path ascending steeply to Rowlings End and the ridge which leads to Causey Pike summit in little over a mile.

3 Continue on the ridge path over Scar Crags and Sail to reach Crag Hill triangulation pillar within another two miles. From here bear 240 degrees initially on cairned path to reach the rim above Addacombe Hole. Follow this round and ascend to the summit cairn on Wandhope. Now head due west to meet the distinctive ridge path which crosses to Whiteless Pike. In mist it is important to avoid being drawn south-east too soon by descending the crest of Wandope and not crossing the gully of Third Gill.

4 From the summit of Whiteless zig-zag southwards down the path for nearly a mile to reach a junction of several paths and locate a small flat cairn. Continue straight on (south-east) towards Red Pike for a further 100 yards to another junction of paths. Here bear left (south) instead of continuing straight on and find narrow stony path which descends steeply towards Ghyll Wood. When opposite top of wood take stony path which bears left and descends steeply to reach gate and stile. Climb and turn right to descend through the wood to emerge in Buttermere opposite the Bridge Hotel.

☐ Toilets, pubs and seasonal cafe

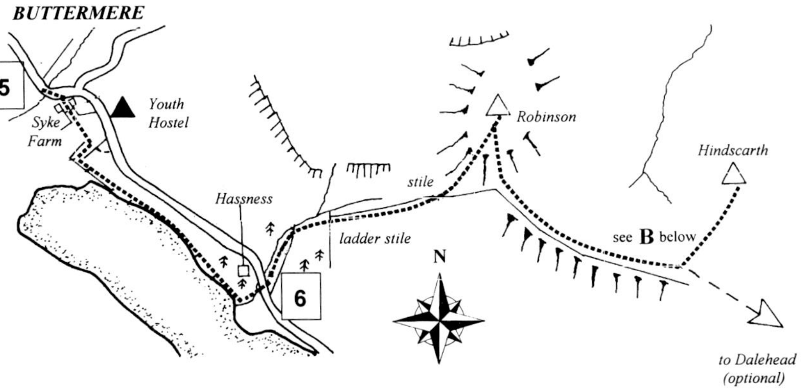
BUTTERMERE
5
Youth Hostel
Syke Farm
Hassness
6
ladder stile
stile
Robinson
Hindscarth
see B below
N
to Dalehead (optional)

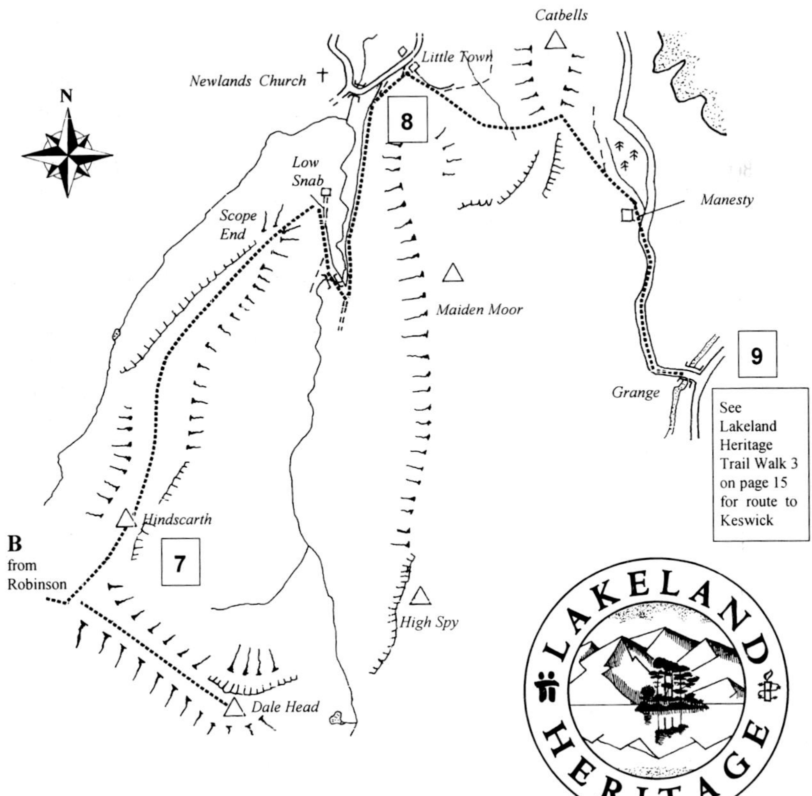
Catbells
Little Town
Newlands Church
8
N
Low Snab
Scope End
Manesty
Maiden Moor
9
Grange
See Lakeland Heritage Trail Walk 3 on page 15 for route to Keswick
Hindscarth
B
from Robinson
7
High Spy
Dale Head

MOUNTAIN TRAIL

Buttermere to Keswick

Allow 9 hours

A lakeside preamble, an unrelenting ascent, airy ridges, secluded valleys and sylvan delights all combine to create a walk of supreme richness, challenge and diversity. A day to be savoured!

5 Facing the Bridge Hotel turn left uphill and shortly turn right at Syke Farm sp (signpost) **Public Bridleway Lakeside path**. Pass through farmyard to take wooden gate. Continue between fences then take track across open field to turn right sp **Lakeshore Footpath** just before another wooden gate. Continue by fence, through gate and bear left to cross beck. Go through gate and take obvious path to the lakeside. Follow path through series of gates to reach the entrance to a short tunnel. Pass through the tunnel and continue on the lakeside path to pass through an iron kissing gate. Before next wall and gate bear left through woods to join the left side of a stream, cross footbridge and take gate onto the road (care!).

6 Cross and take gate opposite, follow path through woods to join right side of stream. Follow to cross stile at wall-end. Ascend steeply, initially with stream on left then bear away to reach ladder-stile at wall. Follow fence climbing steeply for a mile to find a small stile in fence. Cross then continue parallel to fence. When it turns east head north to the summit of Robinson. Retrace your steps south back to the fence and follow east for about a mile before striking north to the summit of Hindscarth.
On a good day the two miles return trip to Dale Head is rewarded with one of the finest views in Lakeland. Just continue following the fence south-east to the imposing summit cairn.

7 From Hindscarth continue northwards along the broad ridge. In about two miles after the final steep grassy descent meet with a fence and stony track. Turn right to follow track to meet broad track from farm entrance. Join and follow wall on left down to wooden gate to cross bridge. Turn left and join broad track for about 600 yards. Look for grassy path which bears off to right. This is at a point opposite a bridge down below to the left and Newlands church.

8 Ascend and shortly join broad stony track from Little Town. Bear right uphill for about 250 yards. Look for broad track bearing uphill to right as track curves left. Take this track and continue ascending on stony track which crosses stream below a small waterfall. Continue bearing right to climb more steeply through rough boulders. Large cairns mark the way. The path becomes grassy as the col is reached. On reaching the main ridge path locate the lowest point where there is a small cairn. Looking east towards Derwent Water head towards a wooden fence which marks the start of an obvious way down. The path eventually meets a broad track close to a walled plantation. Continue down to a wooden gate and stile, climb and descend to road. Turn right along the road to reach Grange.

☐ Toilets and cafes in village

9 The route to Keswick is described under walk three of the Lakeland Heritage Trail - see page 15.

Bad Weather Routes
Weekends in the Lake District are usually planned and booked ahead; only a fortunate few have the luxury of being able to pick their walking weather. There is no merit in turning your holiday into an endurance test so it is important to check the weather forecast before you set out, however favourable the weather might appear. In the event of a poor forecast a number of alternatives are suggested below.

Lakeland Heritage Trail
Unless you have waterproof clothing and boots the best alternative to a wet and uncomfortable day will be the shops and cafes of Keswick or perhaps a short stroll to Friar's Crag. Well equipped walkers should find it possible to complete one or more sections of the route in all but the most extreme weather conditions.

Mountain Trail
This is a serious high-level walk which is exposed to all the vagaries of the weather. The long ridge walk over Rowlings End to Causey Pike and onto Crag Hill on stage one is particularly vulnerable to strong winds and driving rain. The stage two climb to Robinson and the high-level ridges to Hindscarth are similarly exposed. It can take more courage to seek alternatives than to press ahead to original plans - the hills will still be there on brighter days! In the event of poor weather there are three main alternatives.

☐ The lower-level Lakeland Heritage Trail. Experienced walkers should be able to complete this in all but the most extreme weather.

☐ Stage one alternative. Follow the path from Rigg Beck GR 229 202 which takes the valley route to Buttermere between Ard Crags and Crag Hill.

☐ Stage two alternative. Instead of ascending Robinson from Hassness continue along the lakeside path then onto Gatescarth cottages GR 195 149. Follow the path along Warnscale bottom to ascend to the hut at Dubs Quarry GR 216 133 to find straight path which follows an old tramway to Honister Hause. Descend road to track at GR 235 138 and follow past Castle Crag to Grange.

Badges and Certificates - to support the work of Christian Aid and Amnesty International

These are available to anyone who completes either Trail, or any section or stage without the use of private transport. The inclusion of bad weather alternatives is permissible provided a return stage is completed back to Keswick.

Send a 9"X4" SAE with a donation of at least £3-00 payable to *Lakeland Heritage* to:

Lakeland Heritage
10 Beaufort Grove
Bradford
BD2 4 L J

All receipts will be subsequently divided equally between Christian Aid and Amnesty International and paid over annually. There will be no deduction for the cost of producing the badges or certificates. For more information on the work of the two organisations see pages 86 and 87.

Walking Groups
In the interests of conservation, groups are requested to restrict their numbers to a maximum of 20 on the Lakeland Heritage Trail and 10 on the Mountain Trail.

A Guide To

LAKELAND WALKING TRAILS

TRAIL GUIDE

TRAILS

It is only in recent years that the British national long distance footpath has been replaced by the the more succinct American term of *trail*. Routes such as the Pennine Way or Cleveland Way are now called national trails. This trail guide uses the word *trail* in its broadest sense to bring together the network of published routes which traverse the Lakes. Few have any official sanction because the waymarking and promotion of named trails would probably prove to be obtrusive and detrimental to such a compact and sensitive landscape as the Lake District. One of the advantages of more informal routes and guides over official trails is that most are of a temporary nature and are unlikely to leave any permanent mark on the landscape, which is often an unfortunate bi-product of the national trail network.

Most of the walks included in this guide are products of the creativity and vision of individuals and usually it is only through their respective guides that these walks have their being. This has the advantage that numerous and even similar routes can co-exist to give variety and choice without producing confusion on the ground with waymarking or on maps. One of the inherent disadvantages of their temporary nature is that information may become difficult to obtain if the guide goes out-of-print. But you can be assured there will probably be plenty of other ideas and routes to take their place.

The guides can be as varied as the walks they describe and range from free information sheets that give a few key points to define the way to expensive full colour hardbacks. The quality of the guide is not necessarily any measure of the walk itself. Depending on your perspective some of the most rewarding days out can cost no more than a stamped addressed envelope.

USING THE TRAIL GUIDE

For reference purposes the walks have been organised into alphabetical order but for practical purposes they fall into three types based on their distance.

Up To 30 Miles

These walks can be completed in a day, weekend or an extended weekend. Among these are some one day challenges for experienced walkers devised by Brian Richmond of Barrow who has kindly given permission to include the route information.

Under 100 miles

The average walker should be able to complete most of these within a week although many could be completed in sections.

Over 100 miles

Two weeks or more would be needed to do these at a leisurely pace. Again time is not of the essence and the walks can be adapted to inclination or ability.

Key information for each walk

Distance and ascent - are shown in miles and feet as metric measurements have not been widely adopted by walkers.

Terrain - indicates whether it is on clear paths or over open country, high or low-level.

Grade - three simple grades have been adopted - easy, moderate and strenuous. This will be determined by a combination of the terrain, the amount of ascent and the overall mileage.

Maps - The Ordnance Survey Outdoor Leisure maps (1:25,000 or 2.5" to a mile) which cover the national park area are recommended. Elsewhere Landranger (1:50,000) sheet numbers are given.

Waymarking - routes are **not** waymarked unless indicated otherwise.

Publications - these will have an address and price if they are only available locally or privately, others should be obtainable through national booksellers.

Information Sheets - are free, please send SAE.

Route Outline - grid references are generally given for walks of 30 miles and under.

Route Mileage - for multi-day routes the place and mileage is usually given for each overnight stop.

Route Map - these are in proportion although not to any specific scale; their purpose is to give an appreciation of the route and its location.

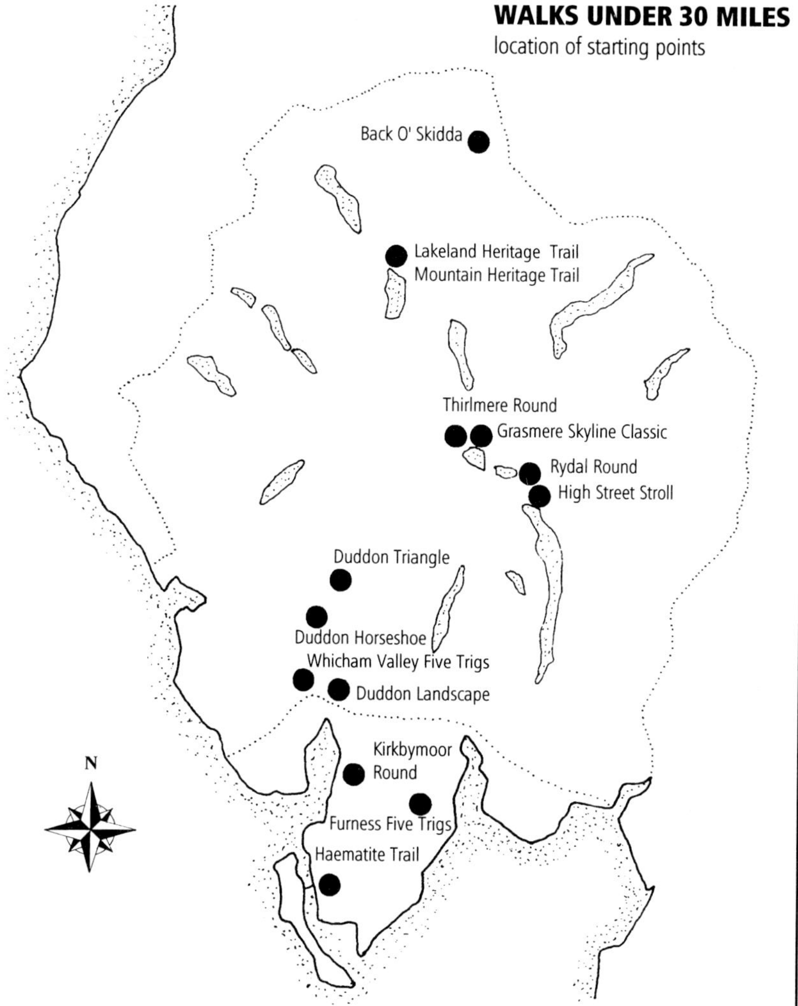

WALKS under 30 miles

Haematite Trail	18 miles	Thirlmere Round	22 miles
Kirkbymoor Round	18 miles	Grasmere Skyline	23 miles
Duddon Horseshoe	20 miles	Duddon Landscape	23 miles
Whicham Valley Five Trigs	20 miles	Rydal Round	28 miles
Duddon Triangle	20 miles	Back O' Skidda	28 miles
Furness Five Trigs	25 miles	High Street Stroll	30 miles

WALKS OVER 30 MILES

location of starting points

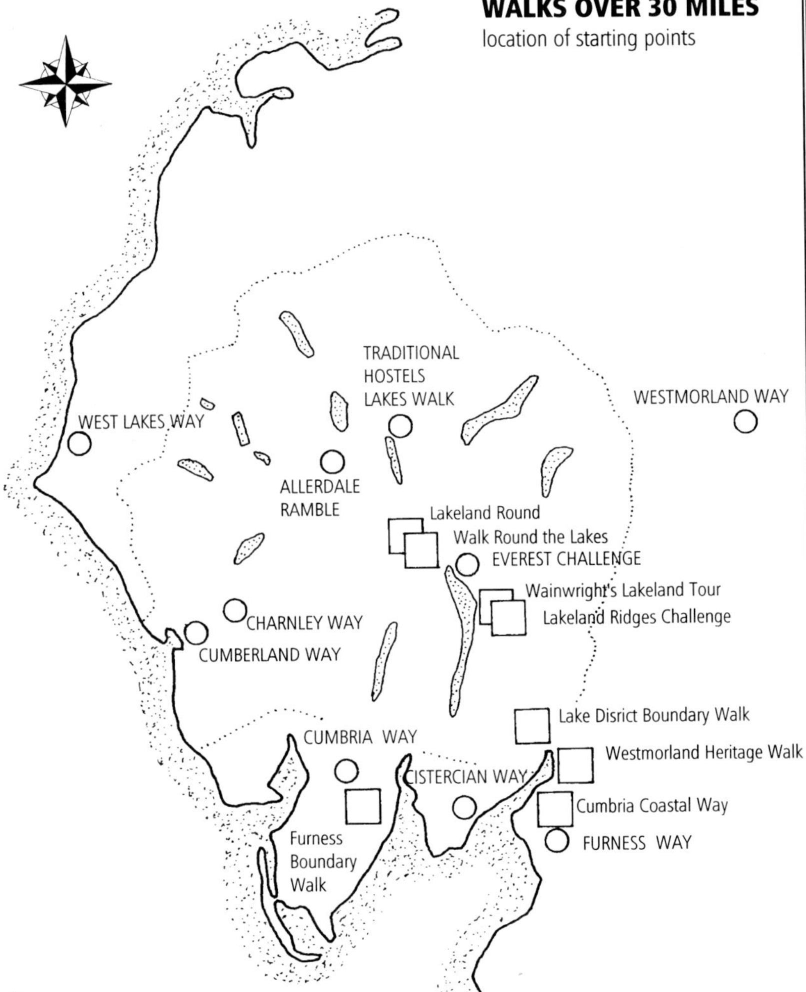

○ **WALKS under 100 miles** □ **WALKS over 100 miles**

WALKS under 100 miles	
CISTERCIAN WAY	33 miles
CHARNLEY WAY	36 miles
ALLERDALE RAMBLE	55 miles
TRADITIONAL HOSTELS WALK	65 miles
CUMBRIA WAY	70 miles
WEST LAKES WAY	70 miles
FURNESS WAY	75 miles
CUMBERLAND WAY	80 miles
EVEREST CHALLENGE	83 miles
WESTMORLAND WAY	98 miles

WALKS over 100 miles	
Wainwright's Lake District Tour	102 miles
Furness Boundary Walk	110 miles
Lakeland Round	125 miles
Walk Round the Lakes	145 miles
Lake District Boundary Walk	152 miles
Cumbria Coastal Way	170 miles
Lakeland Ridges Challenge Walk	181 miles
Westmorland Heritage Walk	200 miles

ALLERDALE RAMBLE

North West Lakes

The contrast between such exalted mountain pleasures and the delights of the broad, flat valley are part of the characteristic charm of Borrowdale. The wealth of the richly wooded crags that hang over the valley, the rattling stony becks like Langstrath that come gabbling down from the mountains, the remoteness from the world that emphasises the humanity of the little villages - these are perhaps definable elements, though the essence remains elusive. Borrowdale is dramatic and yet lovable, and always unpredictable.

Frank Singleton, 1956

Trek from the heart of the Lake District to the Solway coast on one of the area's most established trails.

Start Seathwaite, Borrowdale GR 235 122
Finish Grune Point GR 145 571
Maps Outdoor Leisure The English Lakes - North West , Landranger 85,98,90. The route is marked on these maps.
Grade easy multi-day route described in six stages of 7 to 12 miles, some alternatives available.
Terrain varied - valley, field and coastal paths.
Publications The Allerdale Ramble, Fred Harper and Harry Appleyard, Allerdale District Council, 1986. Out of print in 1997 but may be reprinted in 1998. Enquire at Cockermouth Tourist Information Centre. The Cumbria Way and The Allerdale Ramble, Jim Watson, Cicerone Press 1997.

ROUTE MAP

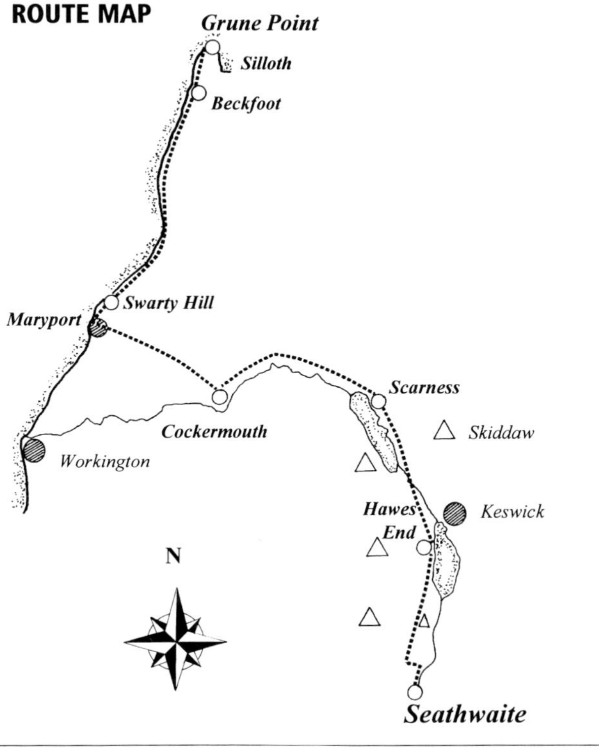

Route Mileage

Seathwaite 0
Hawes End 9
Scarness 19
Cockermouth 27
Swarty Hill 40
Beckfoot 47
Grune Point 55

BACK O' SKIDDA

North Lakes

28 miles

A walk on the wilder side of the Lakes notable for visiting Mungrisedale Common, a patch of the Lakes unloved even by Wainwright but popular with sheep.

Start and finish Mosedale village GR 357 323 - north of A66 Keswick to Penrith road
Maps Landranger 90.
Ascent 7,600 feet.
Grade strenuous, navigational skills essential.
Terrain mostly high fells, rough in places.
Badge and certificate available - no time limit, originally designed as a one day challenge by Frank Yates but may be completed over a longer period.
Information Sheet send SAE to Joyce Sidebottom, 8 Mill Lane, Horwich, Bolton BL6 6AT. Promoted on behalf of the Long Distance Walkers' Association.

ROUTE OUTLINE

Mosedale GR 357 323 - Carrock Fell GR 342 336 - High Pike GR 319 350 - Knott GR 296 330 - Great Calva GR 291 312 - Whitewater Dash GR 272 313 - Skiddaw GR 261 291 - Skiddaw Little Man GR 267 278 - Lonscale Fell GR 285 272 - Skiddaw House GR 287 291 - Mungrisedale Common GR 309 294 - Blencathra GR 323 277 - Footbridge GR 344 279 - Bannerdale Crags GR 335 291 - Bowscale Tarn GR 336 314 - Mosedale

ROUTE MAP

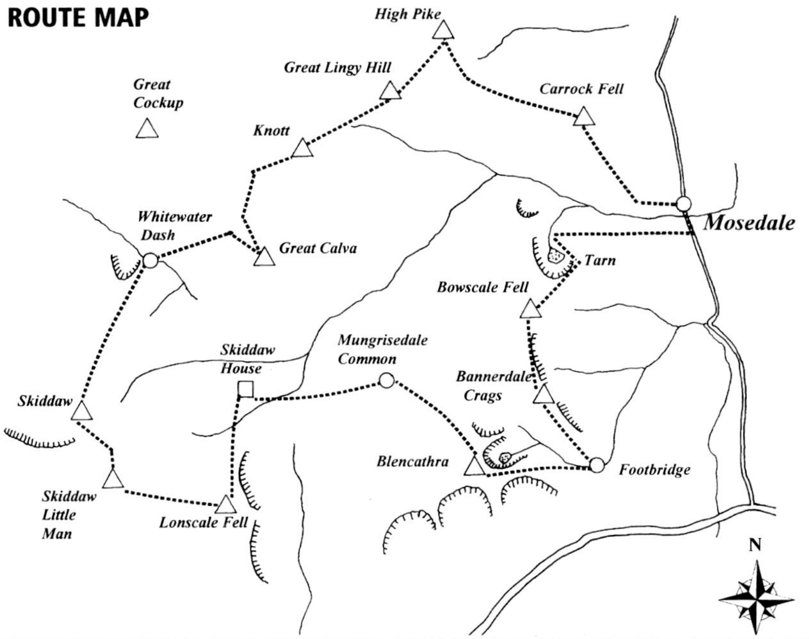

CHARNLEY WAY

Central Lakes

The Charnley Way was devised as a memorial to Gerry Charnley who made a unique contribution to outdoor pursuits in the Lake District. He was killed in a tragic accident in December 1982. The area chosen for this route was the scene of the Karrimor International Mountain Marathon, an event which he devised and organised in 1981.
The route of the Charnley Way has been designed to provide the option of three single circuits or a continuous traverse. Each circuit starts at a youth hostel in Eskdale, Borrowdale or Langdale and converges on Charnley Crag south of Esk Pike.

Start and finish Eskdale Youth Hostel near Boot village GR 195 011
Maps Extract of Harvey map of Scafell & Langdale (1:40,000) included in the publication. The route is marked on the map by a series of control points.
Ascent 10,000 feet.
Grade strenuous, multi-day route, navigational skills essential.
Terrain high level mountain terrain.
Publication The Charnley Way is available from Eskdale Youth Hostel; send £2-50 plus 35p postage payable to 'YHA' to Youth Hostel, Boot, Holmbrook, Cumbria CA19 1TH.

A mountain marathon round the heart of the Lakes that provides both a worthy memorial and an outstanding challenge.

ROUTE OUTLINE - continuous route

Eskdale YH GR 195 011 - Slight Side GR 209 050 - Scafell GR 207 065 - Scafell Pike GR 215 072 - Esk Hause GR 232 081 - Glaramara GR 247 106 - Longthwaite YH GR 255 142 - Tray Dub bridge GR 264 099 - Thunacar Knott GR 279 080 - Blea Rigg GR 301 078 - High Close YH GR 338 053 - Lingmoor GR 302 046 - Pike O' Blisco GR 271 042 - Crinkle Crag GR 248 048 - Charnley Crag GR 236 070 - Lingcove Bridge GR 227 036 - Eskdale YH

ROUTE MAP

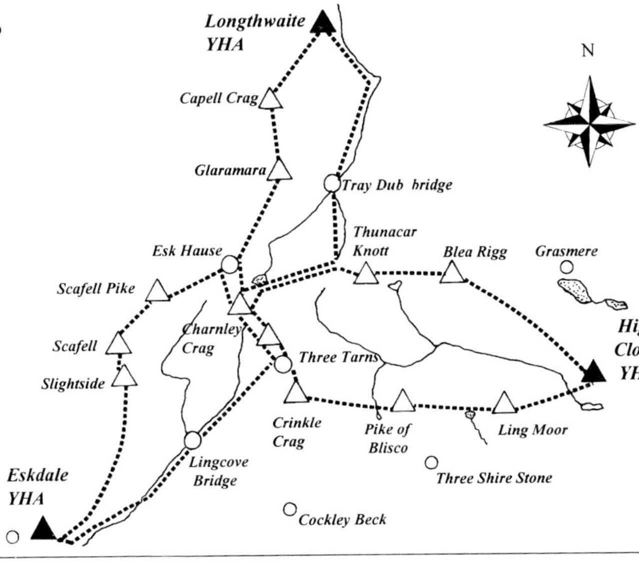

CISTERCIAN WAY

South Lakeland

33 miles

Following the decline of the Roman Empire, the light of the Celtic church and its saints shone brightly in the west and its light penetrated into Cumberland. St Kentigern, St Bega, St Cuthbert and St Herbert all have associations with the Lake District. From these spiritual foundations monastic centres were established. There were the Premonstratensians at Shap and the Benedictines at St Bees and Wetheral. Here in Furness the Augustinians set up priories at Cartmel and Conishead while the Cistercians founded Furness Abbey in 1127.

Start Grange-over-Sands railway station GR 412 782
Finish Barrow-in-Furness GR 200 699
Maps Landranger 96 (route marked).
Grade easy multi-day route.
Terrain low level joining historical sites.
Waymarking walking monk signs.
Publications The Cistercian Way, Ian Brodie, Carnegie Press. Send £4-00 to Carnegie Publishing Ltd, 18 Maynard Street, Preston, PR2 2AL. The Cistercian Way, free leaflet available from Ulverston Tourist Information Centre.

A walk which takes you along the ancient byways of a landscape shaped by shipbuilders, engineers and entrepreneurs as well as early monastic settlers. The Furness rail line allows the walk to be completed in a series of linear excursions.

ROUTE MAP

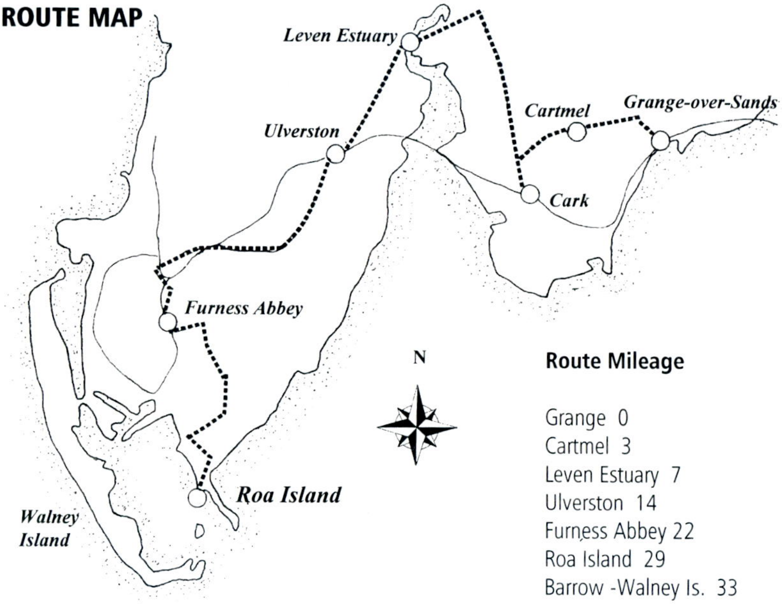

Route Mileage

Grange 0
Cartmel 3
Leven Estuary 7
Ulverston 14
Furness Abbey 22
Roa Island 29
Barrow -Walney Is. 33

CUMBERLAND WAY

Lakeland Traverse

Wasdale

But one element in the beauty of Wasdale is unmistakable. The view as one looks to the head of the valley is the most perfect composition of mountains and water in the district; neither in this country or in any other have I seen anything more beautiful. Being known it remains inexhaustibly new.

F. Singleton, 1954

Start Ravenglass, GR 085 961, village on the west coast on the River Esk estuary, close to the A595 and railway station.
Finish Appleby, GR 683 205, on A66 and close to railway station.
Maps Landranger 89 ,96 ,90 ,91. Publication includes strip maps.
Grade moderate multiday route.
Terrain generally low-level on well defined paths.
Publication The Cumberland Way, Paul Hannon, Hillside Publications, 1985.

This is the first in a triangle of routes linking Appleby, Ravenglass and Arnside in a traverse of the three old Lakeland counties of Cumberland, Westmorland and Lancashire, north of the sands.

ROUTE MAP

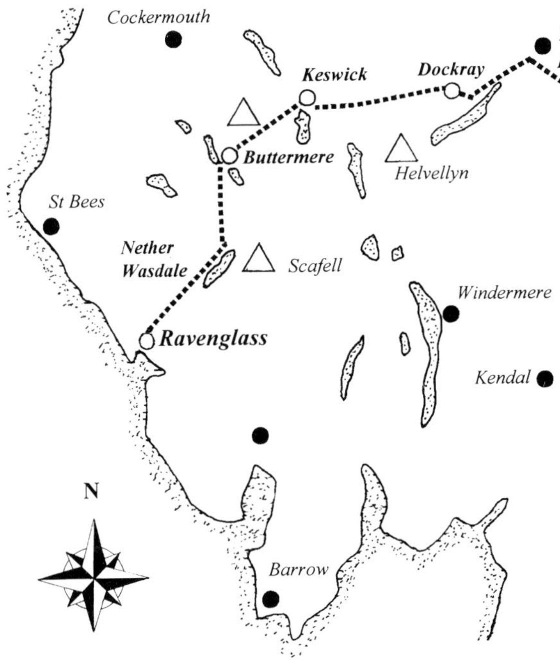

Route Mileage

Ravenglass 0
Nether Wasdale 10
Buttermere 23
Keswick 33
Dockray 46
Eamont Bridge 62
Appleby 80

CUMBRIA COASTAL WAY

West Coast

190
miles

The office of guide has been so long held by a family of the name of Carter, that the country people have given that name to the office itself. A gentleman, crossing from Lancaster, once asked the guide if 'Carters' were never lost on the sands. ' I never knew any lost' said the guide; 'there's one or two drowned now and then, but they're generally found somewhere i'th bed when th'tide goes out'.

Edwin Waugh

Although the Coastal Path provides a continuous trail, it has not been designed primarily for long distance walkers as it can be readily enjoyed in short stages by people of different interests and abilities.

Start Silverdale station GR 475 752
Finish Gretna GR 320 670
Maps Landranger 85, 89, 96, 97.
Grade easy walking, multi-day route described in 16 sections of between 4 and 21 miles although not designed primarily for long distance walkers.
Terrain coastal paths and country lanes
Publication The Cumbria Coastal Way, Ian and Krysia Bodie, Ellenbank Press 1995. Free leaflet describing the 45 mile stretch from Milnthorpe to Barrow in Furness available from the Directorate of Amenities & Development, South Lakeland District Council, South Lakeland House, Lowther Street, Kendal, Cumbria LA9 4DL.

ROUTE MAP

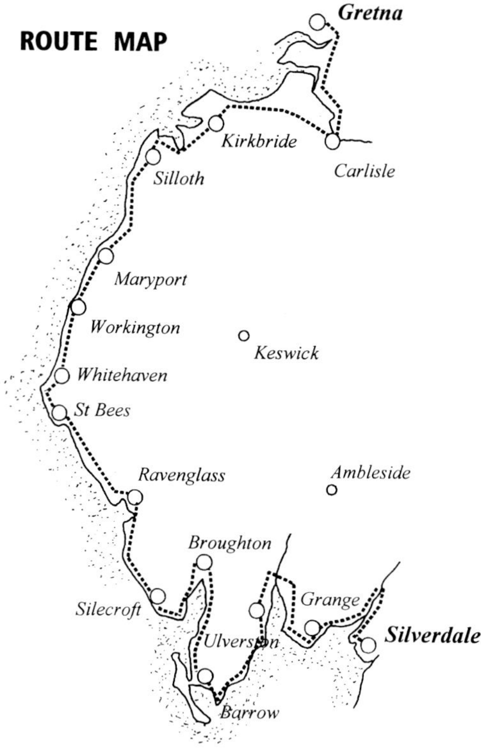

Route Mileage

Silverdale 0
Grange 19
Ulverston 21
Barrow 54
Broughton 68
Silecroft 82
Ravenglass 102
St Bees 117
Whitehaven 123
Workington 132
Maryport 137
Silloth 149
Kirkbride 164
Carlisle 178
Gretna 190

N

CUMBRIA WAY

Lakeland Traverse

Frankly we thought the Lake District dull. I am sure it is lovely holiday country for Englishmen who like walking tours, and mild scenery. Americans however, have enough scenery in the homeland to do three lifetimes. Borrowdale, Derwentwater, Rosthwaite, Seatoller, and the other scenic wonders look pretty pale compared to the Grand Canyon, the Rocky Mountains and the Sierra Nevadas. They have some good mountains in Switzerland too. Why spend a fortune crossing the Atlantic, and wind up by a waterfall eleven feet high? I like scenery (fairly well), but if you are going in for scenery, it might as well be first class.

Ruth McKenny

By world-wide standards the Lake District is not an area of spectacular dimensions. But for compactness, accessibility, richness, infinite diversity and immense charm it probably has no equal. The Cumbria Way offers a well established trail through the very heart of this much loved landscape.

Start Ulverston, Gillbanks GR 284 785
Finish Carlisle GR 400 554
Maps Outdoor Leisure The English Lakes South East, South West, North West; Landranger 97, 90, 85.
Grade generally easy multi-day route, some alternatives available.
Terrain well defined paths through mountain areas.
Publications The Cumbria Way, John Trevelyn, Dalesman 1994. All royalties are donated to the work of the Ramblers' Association.
Guide to the Cumbria Way, Phillip Dubock, Miway Publications. Available from Miway Publications, PO Box 2, Keswick, Cumbria CA12 4GA £3.75 inc p&p. Accommodation Guide £0.60 inc p&p from the same address.
The Cumbria Way and the Allerdale Ramble, Jim Watson, Cicerone Press, 1997.

ROUTE MAP

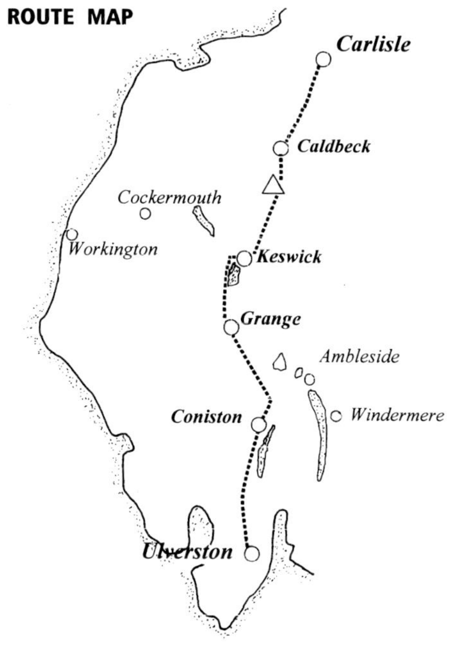

Route Mileage

Ulverston 0
Coniston 16
Langdale 29
Keswick 45
Caldbeck 61
Carlisle 70

DUDDON HORSESHOE

South West Lakes

20 miles

Start and Finish Newfield Inn, Seathwaite GR 227 960 - on minor road off A595 from Duddon Bridge (near Broughton in Furness).

Maps Outdoor Leisure The English Lakes - South West.

Ascent 6,000 feet.

Grade strenuous, navigational skills essential.

Terrain mostly high fells, some rough-going.

Badge and certificate subject to 12 hour limit, send £1-00 and SAE to Brian Richmond, 31 Dartmouth Street, Barrow in Furness, Cumbria LA14 3AS.

Route promoted by Brian Richmond, described by the series of grid references scheduled below.

This is the first in a series of formidable routes promoted by Brian Richmond of Barrow each of which possesses that irresistible combination of beauty and challenge.

ROUTE OUTLINE

Seathwaite GR 227 950 - Wallowbarrow GR 221 963 - Grassguards GR 224981 - Harter Fell GR 218 997 - Hard Knott top GR 232 021 - Little Stand GR 250 033 - Cold Pike GR 263 036 - Three Shire Stone GR 277 027 - Great Carrs GR 270 006 - Swirl How GR 273 005 - Dow Crag GR 262 978 - Walna Scar Pass GR 258 965 - White Pike GR 240 956 - Caw GR 230 944 - Seathwaite

ROUTE MAP

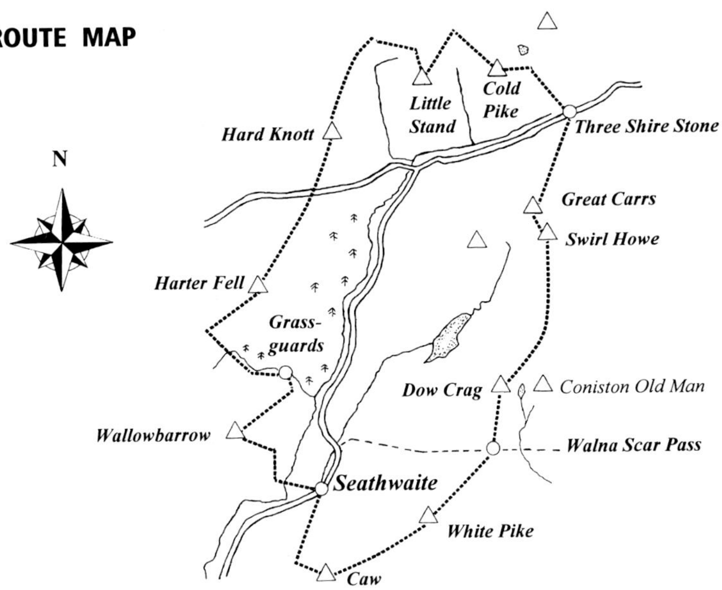

DUDDON LANDSCAPE

South West Lakes

Start and finish Broughton-in- Furness GR 212 875 on A595
Maps Outdoor Leisure The English Lakes South West.
Ascent 6,000 feet.
Grade strenuous, navigational skills essential.
Terrain mostly high open fells with undefined paths, rough and tough.
Information Sheet send SAE to Kate Clarkson, 2 Blundell Lane, Penwortham, Preston, Lancs PR1 OEA.

Solitude and beauty are the rewards for this outing amongst the compelling array of miniature crags and fells that encircle the Duddon valley.

ROUTE OUTLINE

Broughton GR 212 875 - Old Forge GR 197 882 - Buckbarrow GR 152 911 - Whitfell GR 159 930 - Birker Fell GR 171 977 - Gt Worm Crag GR 194 969 - Green Crag GR 200 983 - Harter Fell GR 218 997 - Seathwaite GR 229 962 - Gt Stickle GR 212 916 - Lower Bleansley GR 207 891 - Broughton

ROUTE MAP

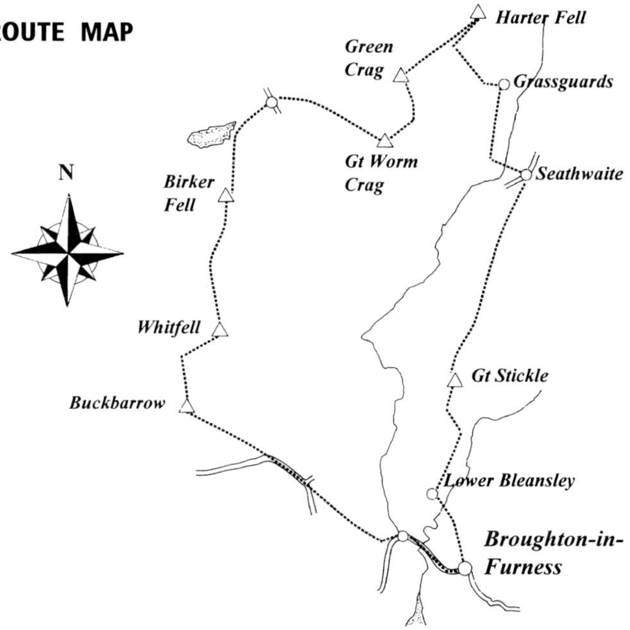

DUDDON TRIANGLE

South West Lakes

20 miles

Start and Finish Ulpha Bridge GR 196 930 - on minor road off A 595 from Duddon Bridge, near Broughton-in-Furness.

Maps Outdoor Leisure The English Lakes - South East.

Ascent 5,000 feet.

Grade strenuous, navigational skills essential.

Terrain high open fells, rough and tough.

Badge and certificate subject to 10 hour limit, send £1-00 and SAE to Brian Richmond, 31 Dartmouth Street, Barrow in Furness, Cumbria LA14 3AS.

Route devised by Brian Richmond, described by the series of grid references shown below.

The sustained interest, beauty and challenge of this corner of Lakeland demands more than a single fleeting visit. It is little wonder that Wordsworth spent sixteen years composing his thirty-four sonnets in praise of its virtuosity.

They can feel its magic as they look down on it from Walna Scar, or from the Parks above Newfield, or from the forest path on Harter Fell; there are some who, straying beyond the church of Seathwaite as far as the beautiful cascades called the Pitchers, feel that they have seen the best the valley can hold; others rushing up-dale on wheels believe they have reached an understanding with the Duddon. But no, they have merely caught the edge of understanding. The more we live with the Duddon the more there is to know. The longer we stay in the dale the more loath we are to go.

Jessica Lofthouse, 1956

ROUTE OUTLINE

Ulpha Bridge GR 196 930 - Bigert Mire GR 179 927 - Whitfell GR 159 930 - Windsgate GR 185 957 - Harter Fell GR 218 997 - Seathwaite GR 227 950 - Caw GR 230 944 - Ulpha Bridge

ROUTE MAP

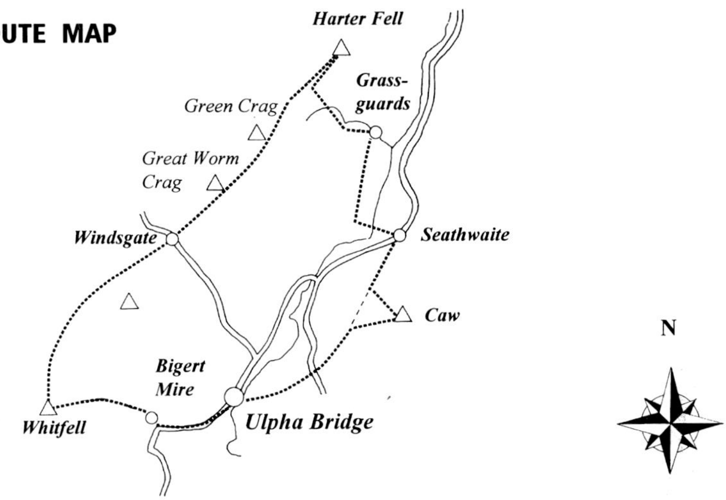

83 miles

EVEREST CHALLENGE

Lakeland Circuit

The Oxfam Everest Challenge was devised by the Northumberland Mountaineering Club on behalf of Oxfam, with the dual objectives of climbing the height of Everest, 29,028 feet, in the Lake District and supporting the poor of Nepal in their climb out of poverty.

Start Ambleside GR 376 045
Finish Old Dungeon Ghyll Hotel, Langdale GR 285 061
Maps English Lakes South East, North East, North West, South West.
Grade strenuous six day challenge described in stages of between 10 and 16 miles.
Ascent 29,575 feet.
Terrain generally well defined paths over high mountain country.
Publication The Oxfam Everest Challenge, Send £5-00 (cheques payable to Oxfam) to Oxfam North West Campaigns Office, 7th Floor, Graeme House, Wilbraham Road, Chorlton, Manchester, M21 9AS.

If a problem seems too great it is good to remember that there is only one way to eat an elephant - one piece at a time.
Archbishop Desmond Tutu

ROUTE MAP showing principal summits

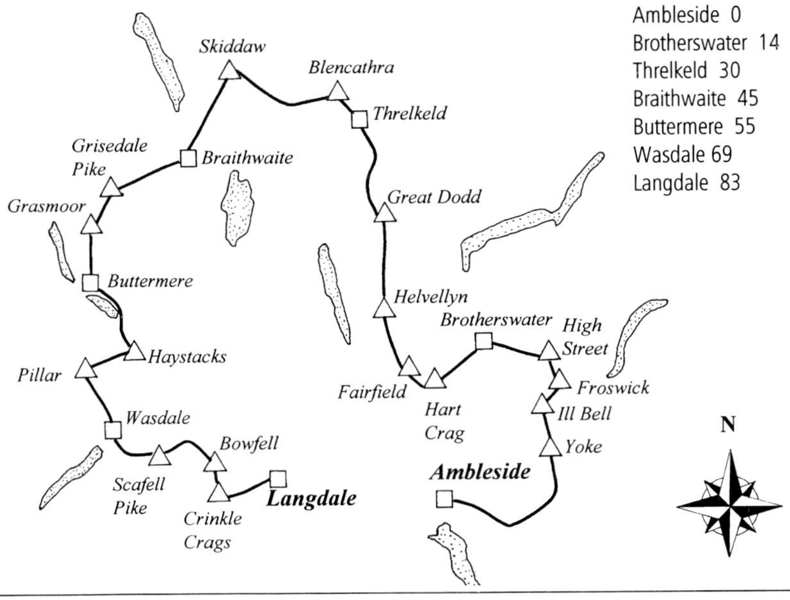

Route Mileage

Ambleside 0
Brotherswater 14
Threlkeld 30
Braithwaite 45
Buttermere 55
Wasdale 69
Langdale 83

FURNESS BOUNDARY

South Lakes

110 miles

History and tradition are interwoven at Aldingham. They say Saint Cuthbert's body rested here when his monks in Lindisfarne sought to preserve it from the ravening Danes, and the church is dedicated to him, though there is no proof the story is true. With Norman times history is more certain. Michael le Fleming was the Norman lord of Aldingham, with a moat- defended dwelling on the sea edge mound south of the church.

Jessica Lofthouse,1956

Although only 25 miles from north to south and some 6 to 7 miles in width it is difficult to imagine an area of greater scenic variety and contrast or greater richness of history. A walk on the quieter side of the Lakes.

Start and Finish Canal Foot, Ulverston GR 314 777

Maps Landranger 96.

Grade easy route described in 29 linear sections of commentary and sketches.

Terrain coastal and valley paths.

Publication Walking The Furness Boundary, John Llewellyn with drawings by Jean Preston, 1992. Produced and sold in aid of St Mary's Hospice for Furness and South Lakeland. Out of print in 1997 but due for reprinting. Send SAE with enquiries to St Mary's Hospice, Ford Park, Ulverston, Cumbria LA12 7JS.

ROUTE MAP

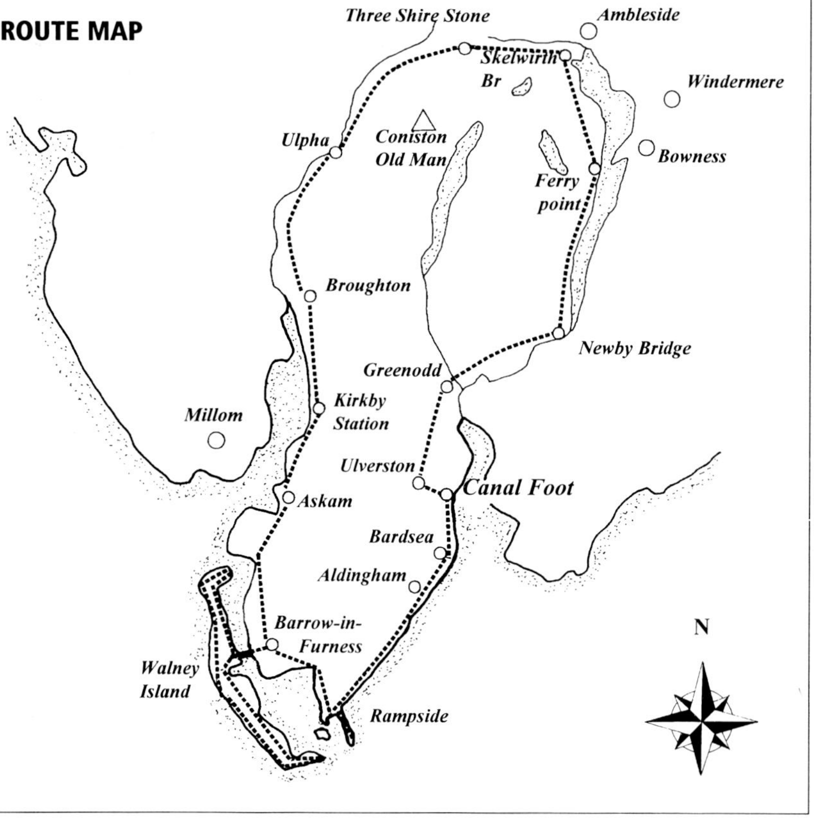

The Hoad monument overlooking Ulverston is a copy of the Eddystone Lighthouse. It was built as a tribute to Sir John Barrow , born in Ulverston in 1764, who founded the Royal Geographical Society and did much to encourage polar and arctic exploration.

Start Ulverston, Gillbanks GR 285 787
Finish Hoad monument GR 294 791
Maps Landranger 96.
Ascent 2,000 feet.
Grade moderate walking linking the highest points in the Low Furness area; navigational ability required.
Terrain varied - field paths, country lanes, canal and open moor and low fells.
Badge and certificate subject to 12 hour limit, send £1-00 and SAE to Brian Richmond, 31 Dartmouth Street, Barrow in Furness, Cumbria LA14 3AS.
Route devised by Brian Richmond, described by the schedule of grid references listed below.

ROUTE OUTLINE

Gillbanks GR 285 787 - Old Hall Farm GR 280 795 - Higher Lath Farm GR 276 803 - Harlock Farm GR 253 803 - **Bank House Moor** GR 245 804 - Stewner Park GR 239 786 - road junction GR 231 765 - **High Haume** GR 226 761 - Billing Cottage GR 227 723 - **Yarlside** GR 231 711 - bridlepath/road GR 242 714 - Scudda Bank GR 245 711 - Stainton with Adgarley GR 249 724 - Bolton Heads GR 256 731 - Little Urswick GR 263 736 - **Birkrigg Common** GR 283 742 - cattlegrid GR 296 737 - Wadhead Scar GR 308745 Sandside GR 305 773 - Canal Foot GR 314 776 - Canal Head GR 293 785 - **Hoad Monument** GR 294 791

ROUTE MAP

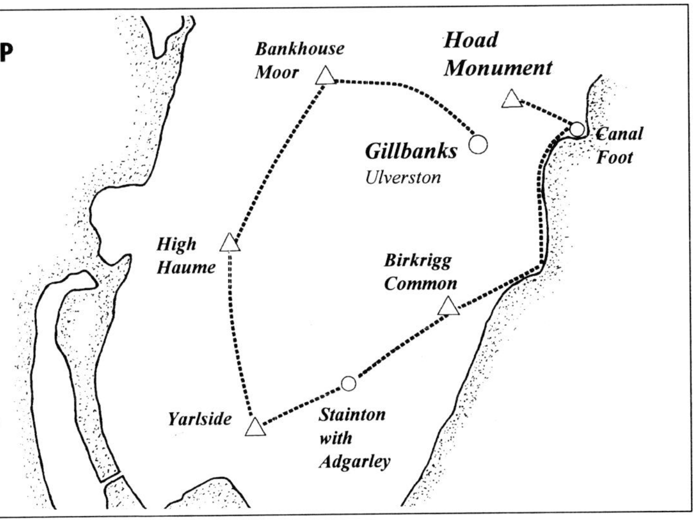

FURNESS WAY

South Lakeland Traverse

75 miles

In 890 a king of Norway, Harold Fairhair, with his Viking warriors and his long ships, sailed to the islands on the west of Britain to punish his rebel colonists in Ireland, but when he landed on the island of Man to do the same there he found it deserted. The rebel Vikings had taken refuge on the mainland, up the wooded estuaries of the Irt and Esk, Duddon, Crake, Leven and Kent. So it was that one of them, Thornstein, came to find the lake he called his own.
Earliest records of the name Coniston are from 1160. It was then Conyngestun, from the Norse meaning "the king's farm". The king may have been Ecgfirth, and the "tun" the place where his men exacted custom from those who came across the sands to take iron from the fells above Langdale.
Almost all the place names around Coniston are of Norse origin.
Thurston - "Thor's stone".
Blawith - "the black forest".
Torver - "the peat water".
Hoathwaite - "clearing in the hollow".
Heathwaite - "high clearing".
Tilberthwaite -"the clearing of the fort of Tilli".
Walna Scar - "the crag of the hawk".

W. Heaton Cooper, 1966

Start Arnside GR 456 787
Finish Ravenglass GR 084 963
Maps Landranger 96, 97.
Grade an easy to moderate six day walk averaging 12-13 miles per day.
Terrain varied throughout ranging from river estuaries to mountain passes but generally low-level.
Publication The Furness Way, Paul Hannon, Hillside Publications.

This is the southern side of a triangle of routes published by Paul Hannon to explore the Lakes in week long trips. The walk traverses the old county of Lancashire, north of the sands, although it actually begins in Westmorland and ends in Cumberland.
The start and finish points of Arnside and Ravenglass offer the convenience of both being on the west coast rail line from Carnforth.

ROUTE MAP

Route Mileage

Arnside 0
Crosthwaite 15
Cartmel 28
Lowick Bridge 41
Coniston 52
Boot 65
Ravenglass 75

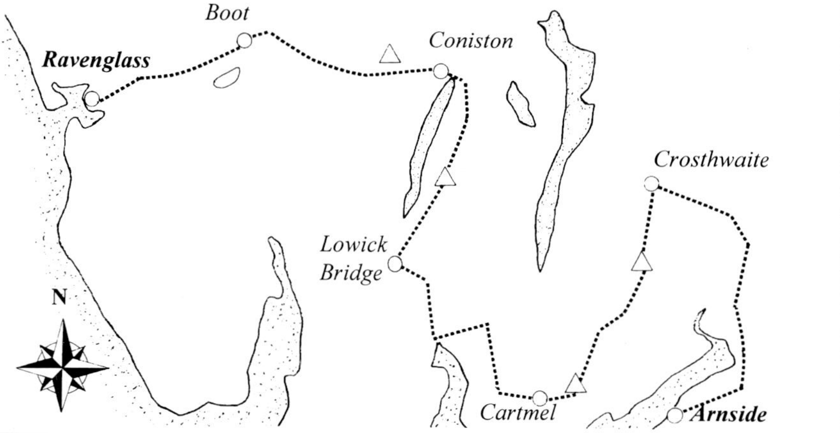

GRASMERE SKYLINE CLASSIC

Central Lakes

This route presents a rewarding test of fitness and stamina among some of Lakeland's best known fells - not for the fainthearted !

Start and finish Whitemoss Common GR 068 345 - National Trust car park on A591 near Grasmere.

Maps Outdoor Leisure The English Lakes - South East, South West, North West.

Ascent 6,000 feet.

Grade strenuous, navigational skills essential.

Terrain high open fells, mostly on well defined paths.

Badge and certificate subject to 10 hours limit, send £1-00 and SAE to Brian Richmond, 31 Dartmouth Street, Barrow in Furness, Cumbria LA14 3AS.

Route devised by Brian Richmond, described by the series of grid references shown below.

ROUTE OUTLINE

White Moss Common GR 068 340 - Heron Pike GR 356 083 - Greatrigg Man GR 355 104 - Fairfield GR 359 117 - Grisedale Tarn GR 348 118 - Seat Sandal GR 344 115 - Dunmail Raise GR 328 116 - Steel Fell GR 319 111 - Calf Crag GR 301 104 - Sargeant Man GR 287 089 - Blea Rigg GR 298 079 - Silver Howe GR 324 066 - Red Bank GR 340 056 - Loughrigg GR 347 051 - White Moss Common

ROUTE MAP

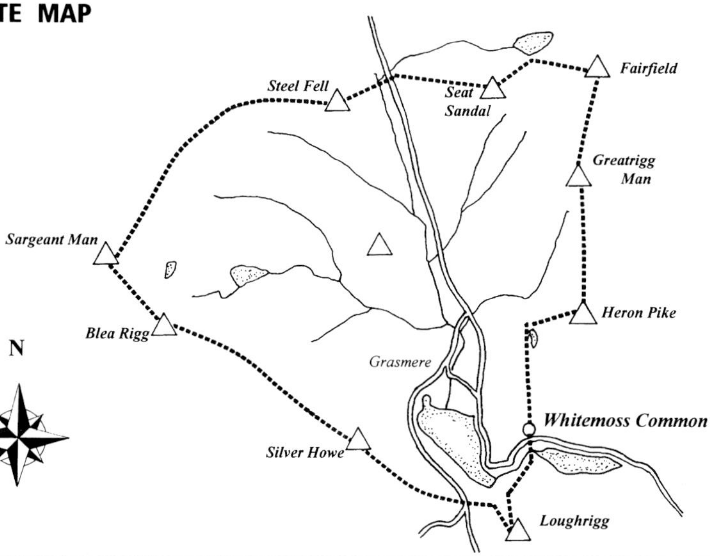

HAEMATITE TRAIL

South Lakes

18 miles

Little Urswick is a quieter neighbour of Great Urswick, with pretty houses and garden walls of fantastic, waterworn limestone, each one a sort of managerie in stone. A few farms, the Swan, and the school stand at the edge of the green where nothing stirs on a summer afternoon except a few geese, and hens scratching for their chicks; sleeping dogs lie. Not far south is Bolton Manor Farm, with an old chapel, first granted as a chantry by Robert Denton, Abbot of Furness, now used as a store house; it has red sandstone mullions, a fine arched door, and its walls are greened with moss.
All around is charming, softly dimpled country, rich fields of red earth laced by green hedges, and very few timber trees.
Go over the limestone pastures beyond Stone Walls and you come to a hollow by Dimple Hole Lane, by Highfield and Standing Tarn, all paths leading to Dalton - and everywhere the redness of iron.

Jessica Lofthouse, 1956

Start and Finish Abbey Road entrance to Barrow Park GR 203 701
Maps Landranger 96.
Grade easy low-level walking, route waymarked with symbols, numerous pubs.
Terrain tracks and field paths and stretches of beach.
Publication The Haematite Trail, free leaflet available from Barrow Tourist Information Centre.

The Haematite Trail has been devised to explore some of the fascinating remains of the iron mining industry which brought about the industrial expansion of Furness. In its heyday the local industry was on a par with the American "gold rush" as Furness Haematite provided some of the richest ore worked in Britain. Along with it came the Furness railway in 1846 and later the growth of the world famous shipyards. The Dock Museum provides a modern visitor attraction which traces the history of these developments.

ROUTE MAP

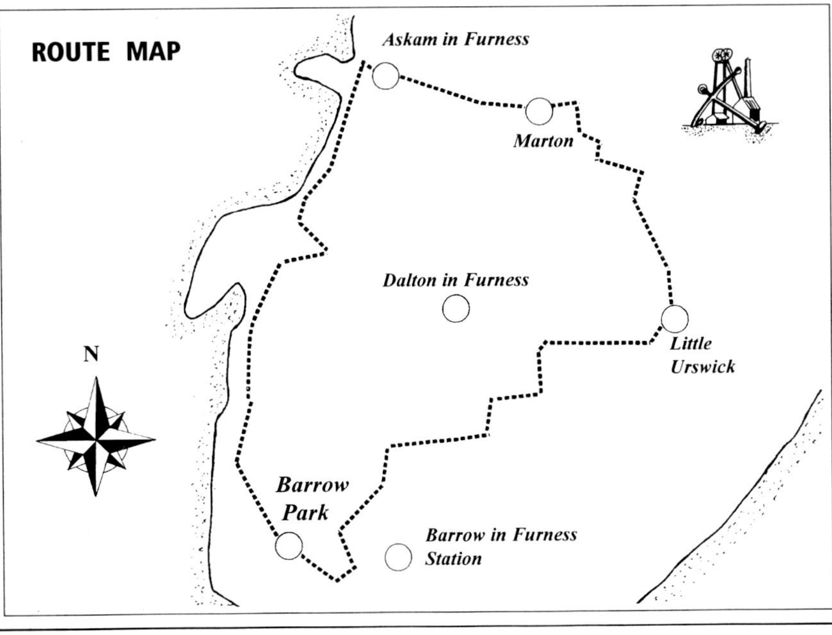

Hamish Brown was the first person to complete a continuous traverse of all 279 Scottish Munros in 1974. The quotation is taken from his account of that journey published in 1978 - Hamish's Mountain Walk .

All men are free under the stars
Yet we bolt our doors and creep to bed.
All men are kings upon the earth
But some have sold their thrones, despaired
and fled.
All men, in Adam walked with God,
Now God and walking both are odd.

Hamish Brown, 1978

Mike Cudahy was the first person to run the Pennine Way in under 3 days. He later set a record time of 46 hours 49 minutes for Wainwright's Coast-to-Coast route.

I can describe the beauty which lies in the endless panorama which will move before me as the day passes into night and the night gives way to dawn, and the landscape continues its almost imperceptible change as I move across it and through it. But I cannot easily explain how it is that at the pinnacle of my physical preparation with all my senses tuned into endless movement and my mind totally occupied with the simplicity of running and walking, that I become more certainly myself and yet also a part of the earth through which I am moving.

Mike Cudahy, 1989

William Palmer was a guide-book writer with a particular interest in the Lakeland Fell Walking Record. The account given here is of Broadrick and Dawson's successful attempt in September 1901 when they completed a round of 67 miles and 16,600 feet of ascent. For a brief history of the record see page 69.

'We went on very well till the top of Saddleback', writes Mr Broadrick, 'the weather conditions being perfect; but there darkness and fog came down together, and we had five hours stumbling along by compass and lantern-light, which owing to the mist, only showed up two or three feet of the ground ahead at one time. Added to that, there was a very strong north-east wind, which blew the light out continually, and necessitated wrapping it up in a sweater. However, after making up our minds several times that it would be necessary to spend the night on the uplands, we struck the railing down the mountain. I don't know whether we got to the actual top of triple headed Skiddaw, but we got to one of the tops, stuck our cards on the caern. It was utterly impossible to tell which of the three it was'. Eventually, at 12.50 after much uncomfortable scrambling and many stumbles, they reached Keswick, and, tired but triumphant, Rosthwaite at 3.04 a.m., thus claiming the record, with half an hour to spare.

William Palmer, 1903

Wordsworth

De Quincey calculated that by the age of sixty five Wordsworth must have covered from 175,000 to 180,000 miles: he still had fifteen years of walking before him.

Morris Marples, 1959

This lovely little lake, this quaint and increasingly tourist conscious village, and their setting in this generously proportioned dale - are these the features that attract so many thousands of tourists to Grasmere each year? Or do they seek the man whose name is synonymous with Grasmere? And if it is Wordsworth whom they seek, is it the man or the poet? Is it the man who crossed to France, to meet and very soon seduce 25-year-old Annette, only to desert her when she bore his daughter Caroline? Or is it the poet, who wrote The Prelude? Or is it he who came with his sister, here to Dove Cottage, to live with her a life which would have caused raised- eyebrows even today, and formed an even stranger triumvirate when he brought too his new bride Mary? Or is it the poet whose "The Daffodils" now turns up in every child's satchel?
We must form our own conclusions, and, in doing so, be generous. For today we are sated with man's imperfections but very short of lyrical stanzas.

Arthur Knowles, 1973

William Wordsworth 1770 - 1850 Born in Cockermouth, educated at Hawkshead Grammar School and St John's, Cambridge. Fell in love with Annette Vallon, in France, who bore his daughter. Lived in the Quantocks and North Germany before moving to Dove Cottage, Grasmere in 1799. Married Mary Hutchinson in 1802 who bore him four children - John, Thomas. William. and Dora. 1805 ascended Helvellyn with Walter Scott, finished The Prelude. Moved to Allan Bank then Rydal Mount in 1813. Visited Scotland in 1814 with Mary and Sara Hutchinson. 1822 to 1846 various editions of A Guide Through the District of the Lakes published. He became Poet Laureate in 1843. Died at Rydal Mount 1850.

To most people today, he is the arch-hiker, the lover of hills and daffodils. It is not, one feels, a reputation that would make a poet popular. Yet a most astonishing thing has happened, as was shown quite clearly during the centenary year in 1950: for Wordsworth has become part of the general furniture of the average modern mind; he has become the stock figure for the poet. It is not that he is read very much, but that one or two of his poems, in particular "I wandered lonely as a cloud", have become the accepted type of what a poem is expected to be. The romantic conception of the poet - the revolutionary, the passionate young man, dying of tuberculosis or getting killed in a battle for freedom - this has been replaced by the figure of an old man at Rydal, listening to the cuckoo and stroking the heads of buttercups.

Norman Nicholson, 1963

Wainwright

I consider his seven Pictorial Guides to be his masterpieces, terms not usually attached to mere guidebooks, but of course these are not merely guidebooks, but philosophical strolls, personal outpourings of feelings and observations, written and drawn by a craftsman and created as a total work of art. It is inconceivable that anyone should attempt to climb and describe all 214 of those Lakeland fells in quite the same way, ever again. Certainly not using public transport to reach them.

Hunter Davies, 1995

Alfred Wainwright 1907-1991
Born in Blackburn, youngest of a family of four. Educated at Blakey Moor School. Became an office boy at Blackburn Town Hall and later transferred to the Treasurer's Department. He was a keen Blackburn Rovers supporter Made his first visit to the Lakes in 1930 and returned for a week's tour with office colleagues a year later. Married Ruth Holden in 1931 who had his only child, Peter, in 1933. They moved to Kendal in 1941 where he eventually became Borough Treasurer. He was divorced in 1968 and in 1970 married Betty McNally whom he first met in 1957. Worked on his Pictorial Guides to the Lakes from 1952 to 1965. The first five were published by Henry Marshall until 1963 when Westmorland Gazette took over. Over fifty other books followed including his Pennine Way Companion in 1968 and A Coast to Coast Walk in 1973. A number of collaborations with photographer Derry Brabbs commenced in 1984 with the bestseller Fellwalking with Wainwright. Michael Joseph (Penguin) took contol of all Wainwright books in 1992. Much of the wealth which his books created was donated to the welfare of animals. His biography, written by Hunter Davies was published in 1995.

You don't have to have an official route to get you into the open air. You don't have to wait for the Countryside Commission to say "OK you can go". You don't have to follow the crowds. In this country there are thousands of long distance routes for walkers that have never suffered an official blessing (and are all the better for that) and any walker with initiative can plan his own itineraries simply by linking the public rights of way recorded on current issues of 1" Ordnance survey maps. There is positively no end to the routes that can be worked out. You may follow high-level tracks over the hills; or circuit mountain watersheds; or march the boundary of your county or any other; or trace old drove roads; or go from point A to point B, whether A or B are called castles, Roman camps, stone circles or whatever; or visit your maiden aunt in Bognor; or cross the country on canal towpaths; or follow rivers from source to sea.
And all on foot, using rights of way, causing no trespass and needing no permission. The map of England is an oyster very rich in pearls. Plan your own marathon and do something never done before, something you will enjoy, a route that will take you to places often read about but never yet seen. You will be on your own unhampered by human beings en-bloc, relying on your own resources to complete what you set out to do. Preferably go alone and do it off your own bat, for it is the solitary walker who most closely identifies himself with his surroundings, who observes as he goes along, who really feels the satisfaction of achievement.

Alfred Wainwright, 1973

Weather

It is no use denying that the English Lake District has the highest rainfall in our island. It is more watery than any district of Clyde. With it even Greenock cannot compete. But what then? The rainfall of Lakeland is one of its greatest assets.
To me when the skies are clear and no mists float over the noble hills that stretch across from Helvellyn and Fairfield to the Scawfell group, they have lost their greatest charm. They do not attract so much. Why is this?
Because it is the mist and atmospheric effects which follow each other in never-ending succession, that give to British scenery the mystery and glamour which are the most subtle attractions in art and literature. Their appeal is deepest of all to us humans who are born and live and die in mystery. When the sky is clear the outlines of the same great hills come nearer to me, as it were; everything is decipherable. The whole secret is proclaimed and, no effort being asked of me, I go home unstimulated in heart and in spirit. My very body does not benefit so much when everything is laid before me and nothing is left to my imagination.
The most subtle of all our sensations, the most lovely of all our poems, the most captivating of all our pictures are those which bring us up against the great shadow - the unknown perhaps the unknowable, who can say!

MacKenzie MacBride, 1922

Yes; rain, and wind, and cloud! Our deities, like the Witches in Macbeth, take their ingredients, and mix and stir them in their mighty cauldron of hills, for ever chanting the words of the refrain backwards and forwards. Cloud, wind, rain! - there is not a month of the twelve on which we can count on anything different. It was of a September that Crabb Robinson after returning from a three weeks' visit, wrote to Wordsworth : " Did I once see a bright sun in Cumberland or Westmorland? I very much doubt it." That was a hundred years ago; and to-day our witches still keep to the old ingredients, still stir them to the same tune, the plain-song of the mountains.

Percy Withers, 1940

30
miles

HIGH STREET STROLL
East Lakes

For some, walking is the nearest and cheapest way between two points: for some it is physical exercise: for others it is an art, a combination of many skills and interests and pleasures.

H H Symonds, 1933

Start and finish Ambleside GR 370 045
Maps Outdoor Leisure The English Lakes - South East and North East.
Ascent 7,000 feet.
Grade strenuous, navigational skills essential.
Terrain mostly high open fells.
Badge and certificate available - no time limit, designed as a one day challenge but may be completed over a longer period.
Information Sheet send SAE to Joyce Sidebottom, 8 Mill Lane, Horwich, Bolton BL6 6AT.

A demanding circuit notable for a visit to Swindale Head one of the lesser known valleys in the Eastern Lakes.

ROUTE OUTLINE

Ambleside GR 370 045 - Troutbeck GR 407 026 - Kentmere GR 456 044 - Nan Bield Pass GR 452 096 - Gatescarth Pass GR 473 093 - Swindale Head GR 504 125 - Mardale GR 469 107 - Kidsty Howes GR 461 126 - High Street GR 441 111 - Kirkstone Pass GR 401 080 - Ambleside

ROUTE MAP

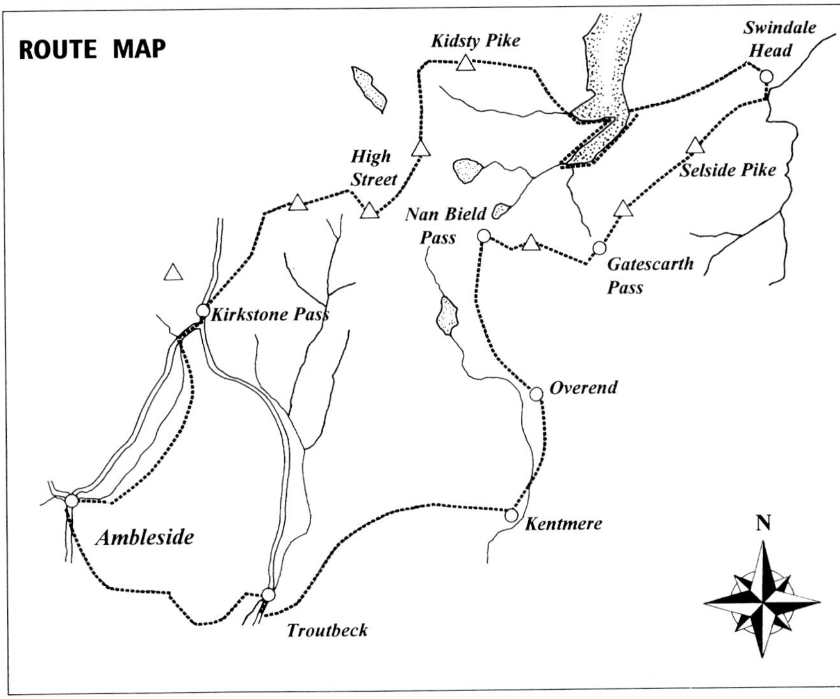

KIRKBYMOOR ROUND

South Lakes

18 miles

Start and Finish Beckside Community Centre car park GR 235 823, off A595 near Kirkby-in- Furness.

Maps Landranger 96, Pathfinder 28/38.

Ascent 2,000 feet.

Grade moderate walking.

Terrain generally rough going over low fell and moor.

Badge and certificate available , subject to 9 hours time limit..

Information sheet send SAE to Brian Richmond, 31 Dartmouth Street, Barrow in Furness, Cumbria LA14 3AS.

Although modest in height this little group of fells offers extensive views. Great Burney provides unfamiliar panoramas of the southern Lakes and the Pennine skyline and is even distinguished by inclusion in Wainwright's list of outlying fells.

Route Outline

Beckside Community Centre GR 232 823 - Winnow GR 250 839 - Grey Crags GR 250 839 - Cocklakes GR 260 833 - Gunson Height GR 259 823 - Shooting House Hill GR 259 818 - Bankhouse Moor GR 245 804 - Crag Height GR 248 815 - Beckside Community Centre.

ROUTE MAP

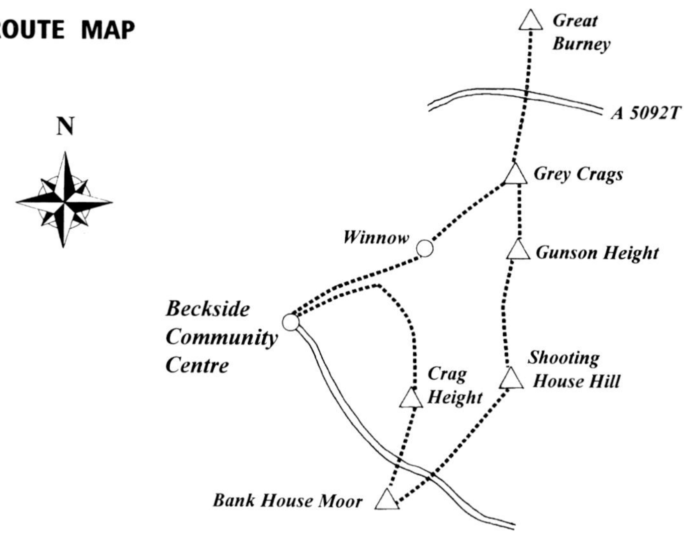

LAKE DISTRICT BOUNDARY

Lakeland Circuit

Although 31 feet short of the magical 2000 that is the traditional yardstick for the conferment of mountain status, nobody can deny this leviathan* [Black Combe] *his true worth as the pre-eminent fell in this relatively unknown corner of the Lake Distict. Indeed, it is often said that the mountain has its own inimitable weather system with locals enunciating the bold proposition that if you can see the mountain, it is going to rain and if you can't then it is raining.

Graham K. Dugdale, 1996

A fresh view of the Lakeland hills and a good way to avoid the crowds; the Lakes from the outside looking in.

Start and finish Gilpin Bridge GR 471 854 off A590 west of Levens.
Maps Outdoor Leisure English Lakes South East, North East, North West and South West plus Pathfinder sheets 627, 626, 625, 575, 576 in conjunction with strip maps in book.
Grade generally easy multi-day route in 15 stages of between 6 and 13 miles.
Terrain mostly field paths and tracks .
Publication The Lake District Boundary Walk, Graham K. Dugdale, Westmorland Gazette, 1996.
Route Mileage Gilpin Bridge 0 - Lindale 8 - Greenodd 17 - Broughton-in-Furness 28 - Whicham 36 - Newbiggin 48 - Gosforth 56 Ennerdale Bridge 67 - Cockermouth 81 - Bassenthwaite 91 -Caldbeck 100 - Hutton Roof 106 - Pooley Bridge 117 - Keld 127 - Garnett Bridge 139 - Gilpin Bridge 152

ROUTE MAP

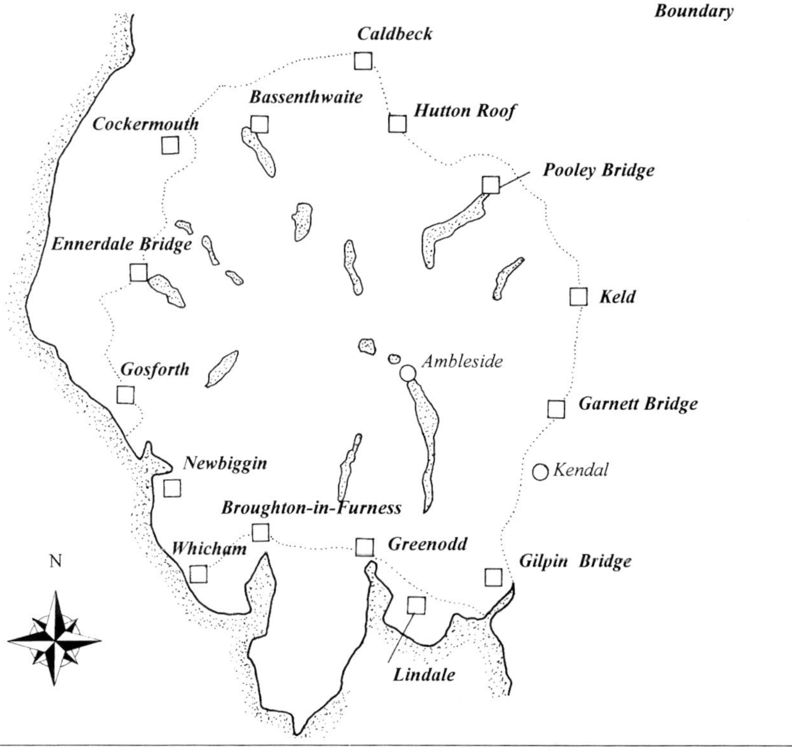

LAKELAND RIDGES CHALLENGE

Lakeland Circuit

181 miles

Striding Edge Helvellyn

A traverse of all the major ridges in Lakeland - probably one of the toughest treks in England.

Start and Finish Windermere GR 412 988
Maps Outdoor Leisure English Lakes - South East, North East, North West, South West.
Ascent 59,000 feet.
Grade strenuous high-level walking.
Terrain generally well defined mountain paths.
Publication The Lakeland Ridges Challenge Walk, Tom Calvert, Leading Edge, 1995. This includes the route marked on to extracts of Harvey's walkers' maps.
Route Mileage Windermere 0 - Haweswater 18 - Kirkstone Pass 32 - Patterdale 40 - Threlkeld 53 - Keswick 67 - Coledale 85 - Buttermere 96 - Honister Pass 106 - Wasdale 117 - Wasdale 130 - Eskdale 137 - Coniston 152 - Langdale 170 - Windermere 181

ROUTE MAP showing principal summits

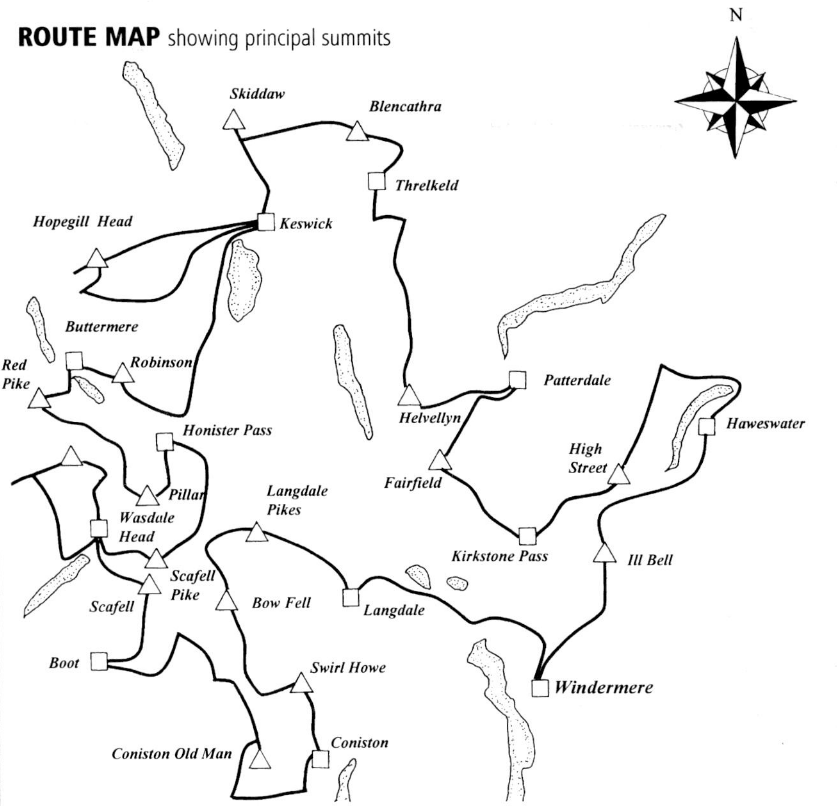

LAKELAND ROUND

Lakeland Circuit

The walk was conceived to link together ten attractively located Lakeland villages or hamlets by means of an exploration of the high fells that would encompass the climbing of most of the major mountain peaks, and of passing through all the different Lakeland scenery, including the rugged Borrowdale Volcanics and the more rounded Skiddaw Slates. The locations were selected on the main criteria that they possessed adequate overnight accommodation in a wide price-bracket, ranging from youth hostels to good-class, medium sized hotels. Each location was chosen for its potential to provide several walking routes - of varying severity but all having interest and variety - to the next destination.

Tom Lawton, 1995

Start and Finish Grasmere village GR 336 076, just off A591

Maps Outdoor Leisure The English Lakes- South East, North East, North West, South West.

Grade strenuous multi-day mountain route described in ten stages of 12 -15 miles with easier alternatives. Navigational skills essential.

Terrain generally well defined paths over high fells.

Ascent 39,960 feet covering 59 peaks over 2,500 feet. Low-level route - 26,710 feet.

Publication Tom Lawton's Lakeland Round, Ward Lock,1995. Accommodation register included.

ROUTE MAP

showing principal summits

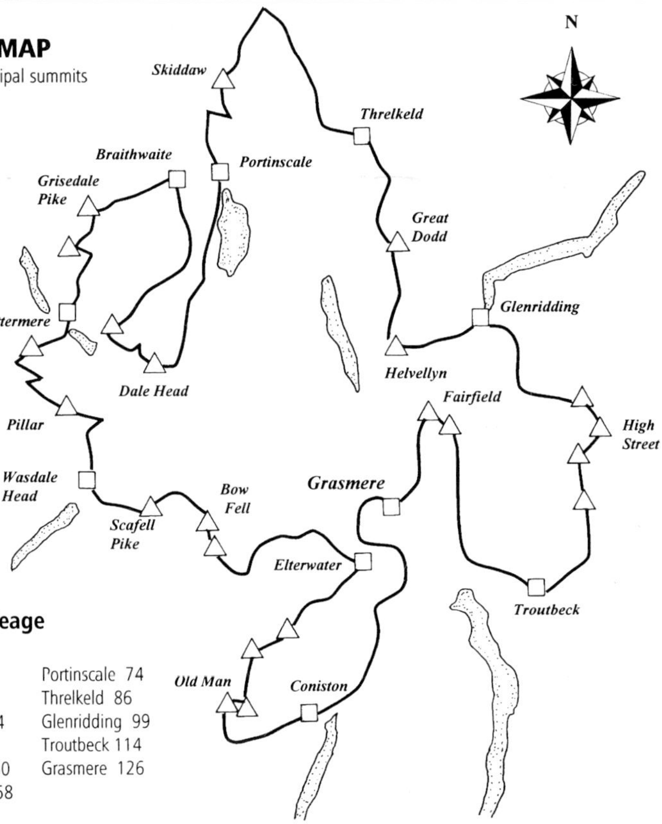

Route Mileage

Grasmere 0
Coniston 12
Elterwater 24
Wasdale 38
Buttermere 50
Braithwaite 58
Portinscale 74
Threlkeld 86
Glenridding 99
Troutbeck 114
Grasmere 126

TRAIL GUIDE

RYDAL ROUND

East Lakes

28 miles

These were the chief of the necessaries which my sagacity procured for our night-bivouac and tremendous ascent: thirty-six bottles of bitter beer, two bottles of gin, two bottles of sherry, one gallon of water, four loaves of bread, one leg of lamb, one leg of mutton, two fowls, one tongue, halfpound of cigars, four carriage-lamps and two packs of playing cards. We also had a large tent which we carried on the back of a horse......At last we reached the top of the humps or aiguilles of Fairfield, a little beyond which we determined to fix our tent. Here we caught the sound of a fowling- piece fired off at Ambleside, no doubt in exultation at our success; and X acknowledged the compliment by tying his pocket handkerchief to his umbrella and waving it three times.

James Payne

Start and Finish Pelter Bridge car park off A591 north of Ambleside GR 365 059
Maps Landranger 90.
Ascent 10,000 feet.
Grade strenuous high level route, navigation skills essential.
Terrain open fells and mountain paths.
Certificate available , no time limit, proceeds in aid of Oxfam.
Information sheet from Jim Strother, Galava Shiel, Borrans Road, Ambleside, Cumbria LA22 0EN.

This is a long day in the hills so follow James Payne's example and do go prepared!

ROUTE OUTLINE

Pelter Bridge GR 365 059 - White Moss GR 349 066 - Alcock Tarn GR 349 078 - Fairfield GR 358 117 - St Sunday Crag GR 369 135 - Patterdale GR 398 157 - Angle Tarn GR 418 145 - The Knott GR 437 127 - Kidsty Pike GR 447 117 - Bowderthwaite Bridge GR 467 117 -Mardale Head GR 469 107 - Nan Bield Pass GR 453 096 - Ill Bell GR 448 101 - Thornthwaite Beacon GR 432 100 - Stoney Cove Pike GR 418 099 - Kirkstone Pass GR 396 088 - Red Screes GR 401 081 - Scandale Pass GR 387 096 High Sweden Bridge GR 379 068 - Rydal Hall GR 365 064 - Pelter Bridge

ROUTE MAP

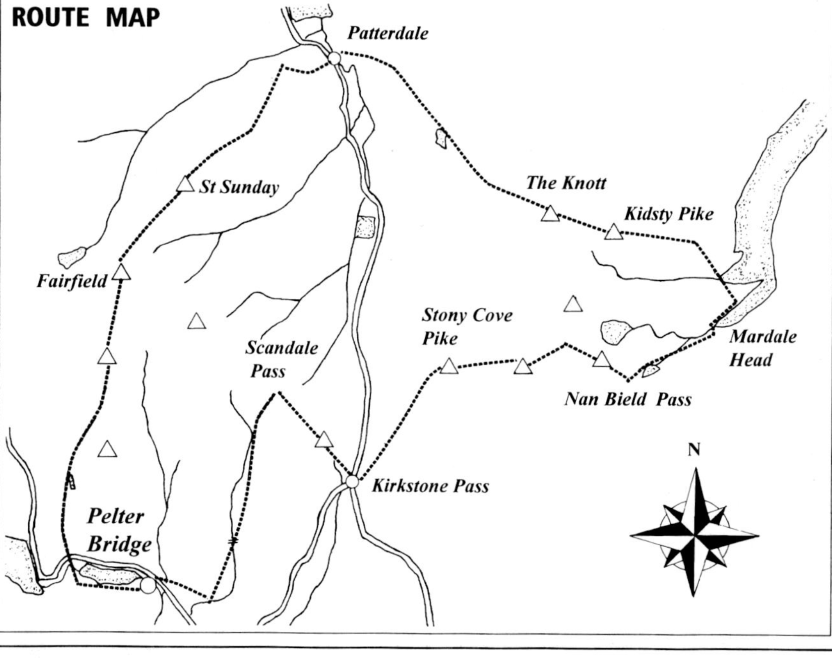

THIRLMERE ROUND

Central Lakes

In dry weather Manchester ceases not to drink and wash, and so the surface sinks and exposes breadths of drowned slopes, a desert, scaly, slimy, bleached belt that hideously encloses the diminished waters. Into it fall, headlong, streams, unnaturally shortened, while beneath it dip lines of old walls, fragments of the old road, sheepfolds, all the network, now meaningless, of man's activities in this great hollow that still, in spite of Manchester, is as a whole so lovely.

E M Ward, 1929

A challenging circuit of two contrasting skylines which offers the rare opportunity of visiting some of the soggiest fells in the Lakes!

Start and Finish Grasmere GR 339 072
Maps Outdoor Leisure The English Lakes - North West and North East.
Ascent 6,800 feet.
Grade strenuous mountain walk linking 16 tops on the Thirlmere skyline, navigational skills essential.
Terrain high open fells, rough, tough and boggy on the west side.
Certificate (no badge) subject to 12 hours limit, send 30p and SAE to Brian Richmond, 31 Dartmouth Street, Barrow in Furness, Cumbria LA14 3AS.
Route promoted by Brian Richmond, described by the schedule of grid references shown below.

ROUTE OUTLINE

Grasmere GR 339 072
Helm Crag GR 326 093
Gibson Knott GR 320 099
Calf Crag GR 301 104
Greenup Edge GR 285 105
Ullscarf GR 291 121
Standing Crag GR 296 134
Middle Crag GR 288 158
High Tove GR 289 165
High Seat GR 287 180
Thirlmere Dam GR 310 189
Stanah GR 310 190
Stick's Pass GR 341 181
Raise GR 343 174
Whiteside GR 337 166
Helvellyn Lwr Man GR 337 155
Helvellyn GR 341 151
Nethermost Pike GR 343 141
Dollywagon Pike GR 346 130
Grisedale Tarn GR 346 118
Seat Sandal GR 344 115
Grasmere GR 339 072

ROUTE MAP

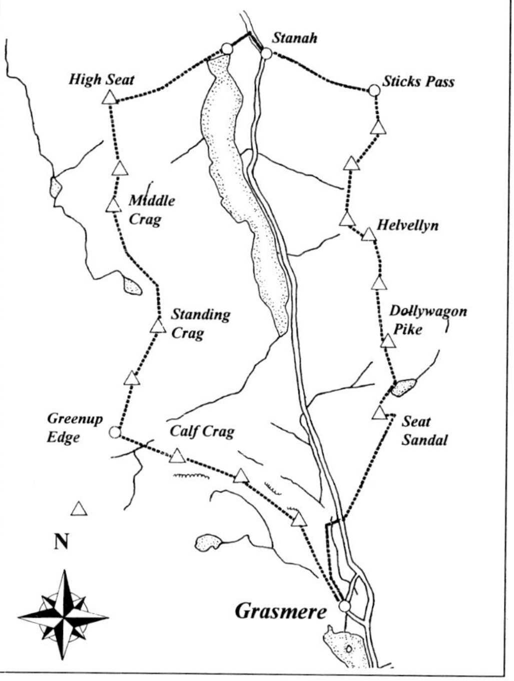

TRADITIONAL HOSTELS LAKES WALK

North Lakeland Circuit

65 miles

In these days of indoor and mechanised life man is beginning to realise that he is in danger of being ensnared and enslaved by his mode of living and by the power and prodigality of his inventions. He longs for contrast: longs to escape from the artificial to the natural order of things; longs to free himself from mass suggestion and mass hypnotism, from narrow diehard, social and political creeds and dogmas, and rejuvenate himself; to seek in purer airs, amid the grandeurs and beauties of Nature, a physical well-being, a mental solace and spiritual expansion.

Frank S Smythe, 1935

This is a route for those who know that our desire for the simple and natural is much more than a romantic escape or a nostalgia for the traditions of another era. A rare opportunity awaits those who wish to avoid the tourist honey pots, and to eat, sleep and walk among the fells and discover something of their secrets. Altogether a true Lakeland experience that cannot be packaged and marketed.

Start and Finish Thirlmere Youth Hostel GR 318 190, off A591 south east of Keswick.
Maps Lake District Tourist Map in conjunction with strip maps in publication.
Grade moderate route .
Terrain generally valley paths and tracks.
Publication The Traditional Hostels Lakes Walk, Martyn Hanks, YHA, 1996. Available from YHA Northern England, PO Box 11, Matlock, Derbyshire DE4 2XA price £2-00 inc p&p, cheques payable to 'YHA'.

Route Mileage

Thirlmere 0
Carrock Fell 13
Skiddaw House 20
Cockermouth 35
Ennerdale 51
Honister 58
Thirlmere 65

Black Sail Hostel

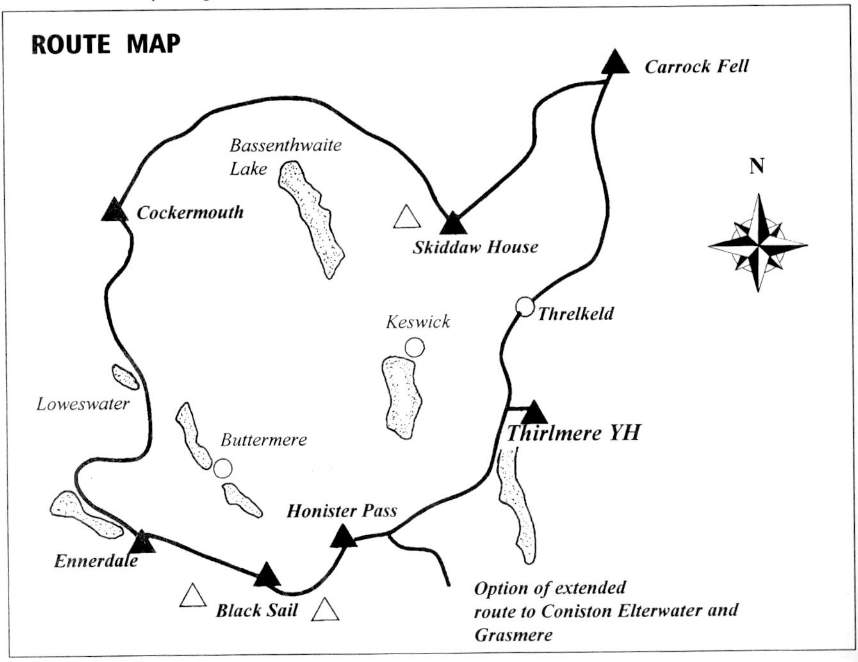

102 miles

WAINWRIGHT'S LAKE DISTRICT TOUR

Lakeland Circuit

A 24 year-old Wainwright devised this route in 1931 for a visit with his work colleagues. His objective was a comprehensive tour to see every lake, every valley and every mountain in the Lakes. This was only his second trip and like most of us his plans were over-ambitious. His six day schedule is an arduous challenge and few fit and experienced fellwalkers would be capable of achieving it even in good weather. The party got off to a late start on their first day from Windermere in appalling weather and abandoned Patterdale in favour of Troutbeck. They later left out the climbs over Blencathra, Grasmoor and Pillar but still managed to complete a respectable circuit.

Start and Finish Windermere GR 413 987

Maps Lake District Tourist Map in conjunction with Wainright's Pictorial Guides.

Ascent 34,850 feet.

Grade strenuous high level route.

Terrain mostly good mountain paths.

Publication Wainwright's Tour in the Lake District, Michael Joseph, 1993.

Route Mileage

Windermere 0 - Patterdale 16 - Keswick 36 - Buttermere 55 - Wasdale 73 Langdale 88 - Windermere 103

ROUTE MAP showing principal summits

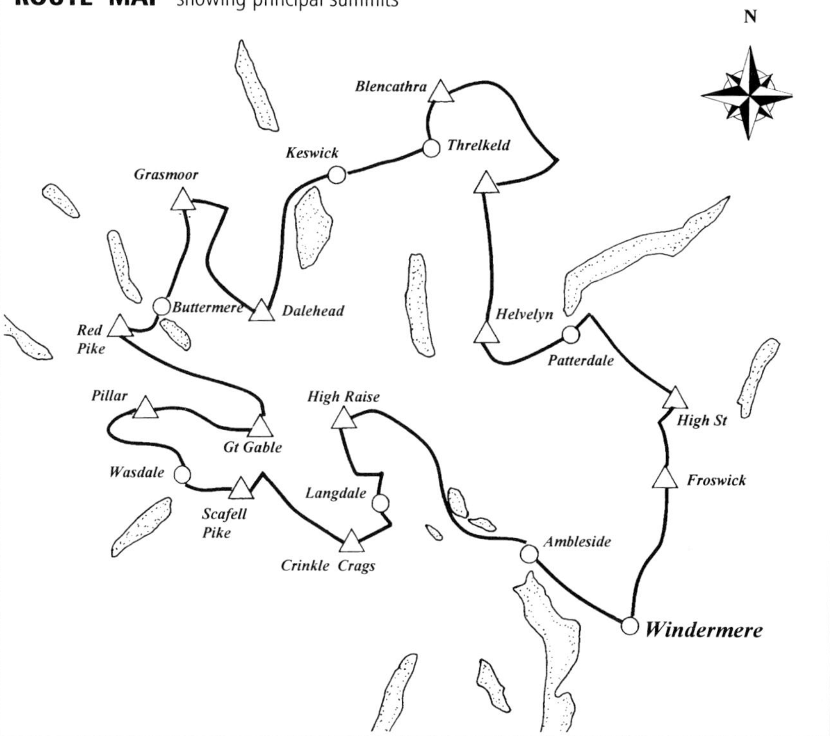

TRAIL GUIDE

WALK ROUND THE LAKES

Lakeland Circuit

145 miles

The Bob Graham Round of 42 peaks (see page 68) was the inspiration for this Lakeland circuit. The basic round has been enlarged so as to visit all the major groups of fells in the Lakes. This has created a 15 day walk with the option of splitting it into two separate weeks by use of a link between Rosthwaite and Grasmere. There is a low-level alternative for each section in the event of bad weather which totals 108 miles. A handy but comprehesive guide book with maps, sketches and route commentary makes an ideal companion to the attractions of this walk.

Start and Finish Grasmere vllage, off A

Maps Lake District Tourist Map in combination with strip maps in the book.

Ascent 49,000 feet high level, 19,000 feet on low level alternative.

Grade strenuous high level route, navigation skills essential.

Terrain open fells and mountain paths.

Publication Walking Round the Lakes, John and Anne Nuttall, Cicerone, 1992.

Route Mileage

Grasmere 0 - Troutbeck 13 - Patterdale 26 - Glenridding 33 - Threlkeld 41 - Keswick 53 - Buttermere 65 - Honister 72 - Rosthwaite 82 - Black Sail 88 - Wasdale Head 97 - Eskdale 106 - Great Langdale 117 - Coniston 125 - Elterwater 134 - Grasmere 145

ROUTE MAP showing principal summits

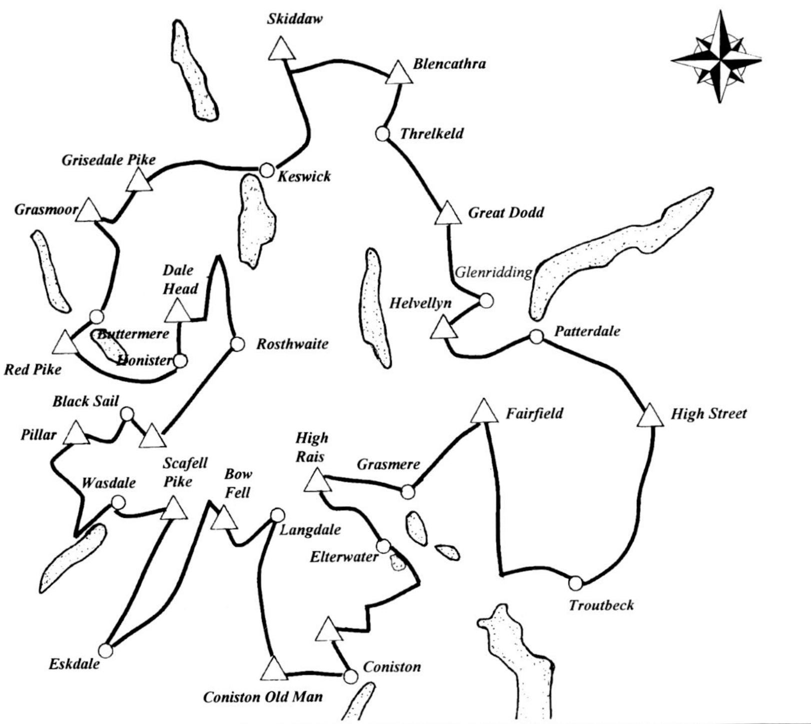

WEST LAKES WAY

West Lakeland

Pillar from Ennerdale

Many might argue that the best of the Lakes is in the west and this route which meanders through Ennnerdale, Wasdale, Eskdale and Dunnnerdale offers a convincing case. Certainly those with a taste for remote mountain scenery will not be disappointed. The start and finish points are convenient for the west coast rail line.

Start Whitehaven GR 973 182
Finish Hodbarrow point, Millom GR 183 780
Maps Landranger 89, 96.
Ascent 15,000 feet.
Grade strenuous in mountain sections, navigation skills essential. Low level alternatives to mountain sections.
Terrain varied - coastal, valley and mountain paths.
Publications The West Lakes Way, Stuart Burgess. Send £1-00 (payable to Copeland B.C) to Copeland Borough Council, The Beacon, West Strand, Whitehaven, Cumbria CA28 7LY .
Accommodation Guide - Cumbria Western Lakes & Coast free from the same address.

ROUTE MAP

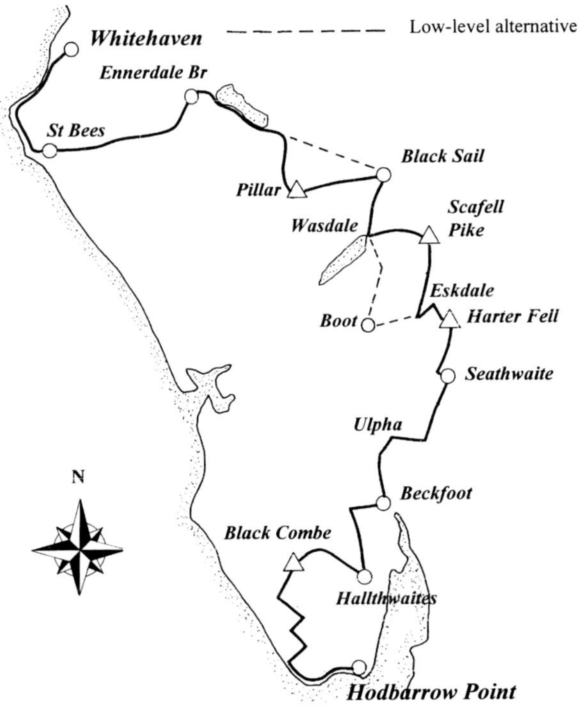

Route Mileage

Whitehaven 0
Ennerdale Bridge 15
Wasdale Head 28
Eskdale 38
Hallthwaites 56
Hodbarrow Point 70

WESTMORLAND HERITAGE

Lakeland - Pennine Circuit

200 miles

Another powerful cause of the transformation of Westmoreland was the discovery of the Lakes, and the consequent flow of tourists, which has steadily been increasing. The love of wild scenery was indeed a discovery for the average Englishman at the end of the last century. Before that time taste demanded trimness and neatness, or at least the appearance of sylvan or pastoral scenes. The general impression left on travellers in the Lake Country was one of discomfort; and the badness of the roads and general inaccessibility of the country did not invite many visitors. The first who brought its charms to public notice was a Roman Catholic priest of the name of West, who published in 1779 a Guide to the Lakes, the first in an infinite series which succeed one another every year. It required the affluence as well as the bustle of an industrial civilisation to create the taste for travelling to out of the way places. Our forefathers did not find the need, which is now so universal, of change of air and scene.

Mandell Creighton, 1897

Start Arnside GR 461 788

Finish Grange-over-Sands GR 412 782

Maps Landranger 97, 98, 91, 90.

Grade multi-day route desribed in 10 stages, option of high and low-level routes

Terrain varied circuit of Lakeland and Pennine fells and dales.

Publication The Westmorland Heritage Walk, Mark Richards and Christopher Wright, Cicerone Press, 1987.

Route Mileage

Arnside 0 - Kirkby Lonsdale 18 - Sedbergh 32 - Kirkby Stephen 66 - Appleby 80 - Brougham 111 - Patterdale 127 - Skelwith Bridge 153 - Longsledale 170 - Kendal 180 - Grange-over-Sands 200.

A celebration of the historical and scenic heritage of an ancient county in a route that captures some of the best of the Lakeland and Pennine hills and dales.

ROUTE MAP

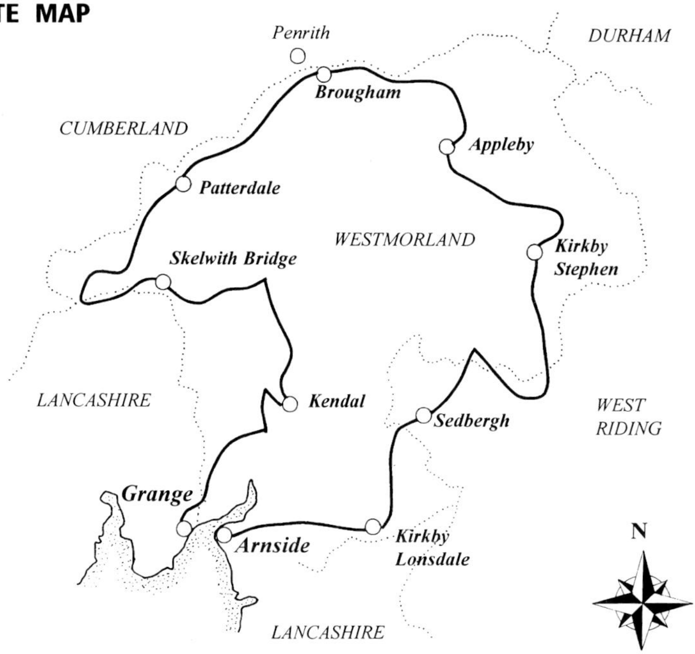

98 miles

WESTMORLAND WAY

Lakeland Traverse

Ullswater - This lake disputes with Windermere and Derwentwater the sovereignty of the English Lakes, and those who find the nearest approach to their ideal of what a Lake should be in the lakes of Switzerland, or even in the most famous of the lochs of Scotland will probably give their vote to Ullswater. Not that it is in any way a servile copy of its larger sisters at home and abroad. It has a beauty of its own which will not suffer from comparisons with any of them, but in its essential features is cast in the same mould. As we sail up one after another of its three reaches, we receive a distinct impression of the individual beauty of each and feel that we are working up to a climax: but there is always something which suggests to the experienced tourist a recollection of what he has seen before.

M J B Baddeley

Start Appleby GR 089 198
Finish Arnside GR 455 787
Maps Landranger 90, 91, 97.
Grade mostly moderate.
Terrain generally well defined paths and tracks, some high fells.
Publication The Westmorland Way, Paul Hannon, Hillside Publications.

This walk concludes Paul Hannon's triangle of routes between Arnside, Ravenglass and Appleby that commemorate the passing of the three old Lakeland counties in 1974 when Cumbria was created. The other two walks are the Cumberland Way and the Furness Way.

ROUTE MAP

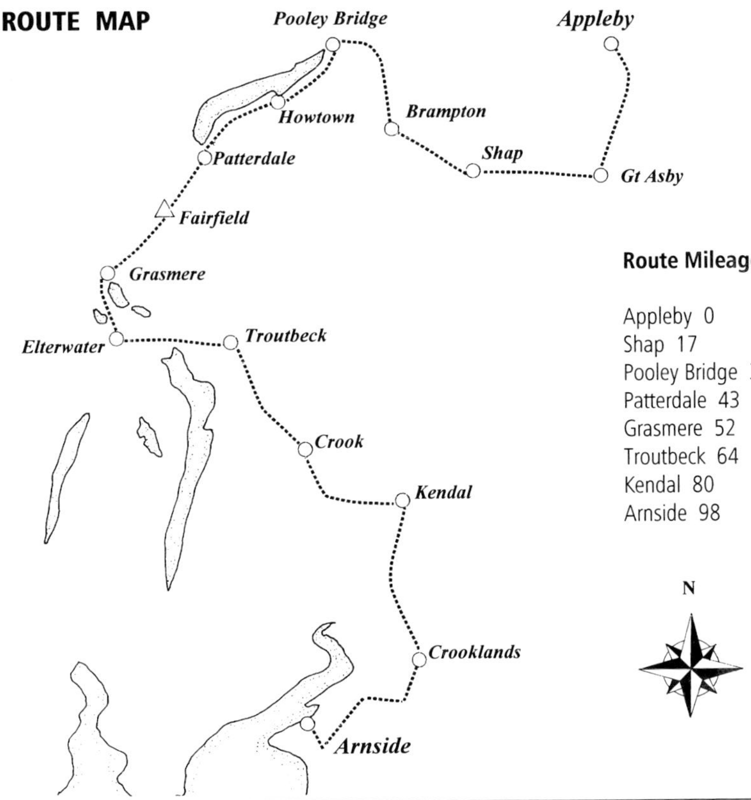

Route Mileage

Appleby 0
Shap 17
Pooley Bridge 30
Patterdale 43
Grasmere 52
Troutbeck 64
Kendal 80
Arnside 98

WHICHAM VALLEY FIVE TRIGS

South Lakes

20
miles

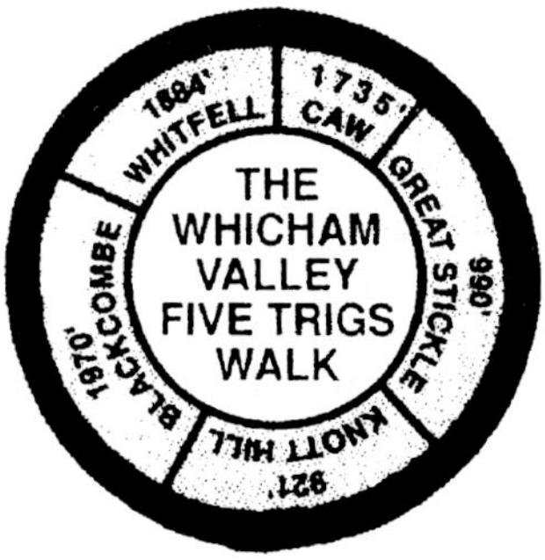

A circuit of some of the great little mountains of the Lakes that make up in character what they lack in height.

Start and Finish Duddon Bridge GR 199 882, on A595 west of Broughton in Furness.
Maps Outdoor Leisure English Lakes - South West.
Ascent 5,000 feet.
Grade strenuous, navigation skills essential.
Terrain rough open fells.
Badge subject to 9 hours time limit. Send £1-00 and SAE to Brian Richmond , 31 Dartmouth Street, Barrow in Furness, Cumbria LA14 3AS.
Route devised by Brian Richmond,described by the grid references scheduled below.

ROUTE OUTLINE

Duddon Bridge GR 188 874 - Beckbank Farm GR 183 868 - **Knott Hill** GR 174 873 - Stoupdale Crags GR 154 874 - **Black Combe** GR 135 854 - Stoneside Hill GR 146 892 - fell rd GR 149 896 - Buck Barrow GR 152 911 - **Whitfell** GR 159 930 - Bigert Mire GR 179 926 - Millbrow GR 188 924 - Ulpha Bridge GR 196 930 - Birks GR 200 929 - Kiln Bank Cross GR 215 932 - Park Head Road GR 218 935 - **Caw** GR 230 944 - **Great Stickle** GR 212 916 - Pickthall Ground GR 209 905 - Duddon Bridge

ROUTE MAP

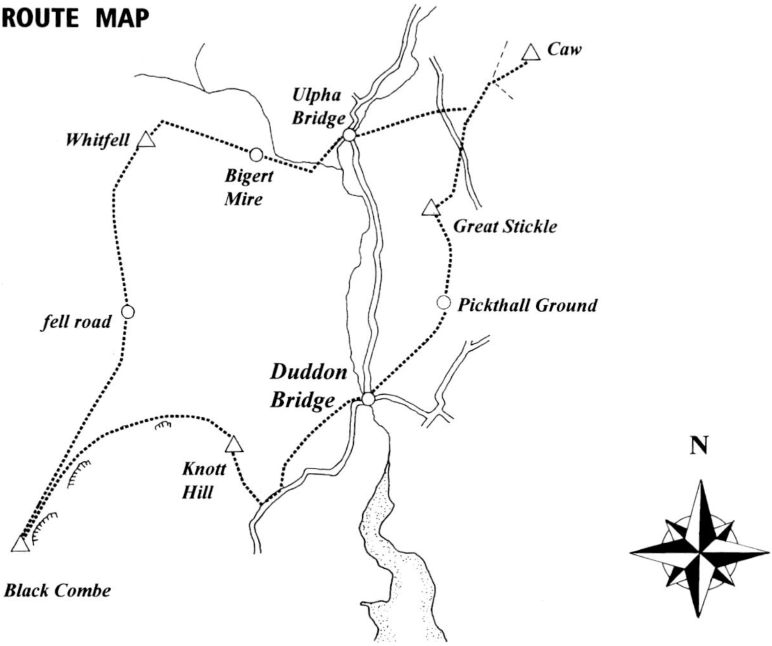

Some of the routes outlined in this section are relatively old and may be out of print. Copies may be available through libraries or second-hand bookshops.

ANCIENT WAYS OF LAKELAND

120 miles
Richard Sale and Arthur Lees, Andre Deutsch, 1986
A valley and passes route divided into twelve lake to lake sections of 6-15 miles with a return route. Moderate walking with the object of exploring Lakeland history and scenery.

CUMBRIAN CLASSIC TRIDENT WALK

100 miles
Jonathan Ginesi, John Siddall Printers, 1980
This strenuous route consists of a framework of grid references with the object of completing a one hundred mile high-level route in five sections. It is called the trident because it traverses the three highest peaks of Scafell, Helvellyn and Skiddaw.

LAKELAND FRINGE

147 miles
R H Gambles and B Richardson,
A G Publications, 1989
A circuit from Newby Bridge that visits some of the less frequented areas on the fringe of the national park.

FURNESS TRAIL

73 miles
Tim Cappelli, Sigma Leisure, 1993
A walk and tour exploration of southern Lakeland connecting the towns of Kendal, Levens, Cartmel, Newby Bridge, Ulverston, Coniston and Bowness.

FOOTPATH TOURING

60 miles
Ken Ward, Jarrold Colour Publications, 1985
A linear route from Ravenglass to Windermere described in eight stages of between 5 and 11 miles with the option of some high-level alternatives. Moderate walking on generally well defined paths.

LAKES LINK

128 miles
Mike Dixon, Dalesman, 1984
A route linking together all the major lakes. Starting and finishing in Ambleside the route is described in 14 stages of 6-14 miles.

LAKELAND TOP TEN

57 miles 30,100 ' ascent
Brian Smailes, Challenge Publications, 1997. P.O. Box No. 132, Barnsley, S71 5YZ
This recently published guide throws down a gauntlet to walk the following ten peaks:
Helvellyn 3,117 - Catstyecam 2,920 -
Nethermost Pike 2,923 - Bowfell 2,959 -
Great End 2,959 - Scafell Pike 3,208 -
Scafell 3,163 - Pillar 2,926 -
Great Gable 2,949 - Skiddaw 3,054
The route may be completed as a circular walk or in four individual sections. Badge and certificate available.

John Merrill's
LAKELAND CHALLENGE

18 miles
John Merrill, Footprint Publications
A strenuous circuit of ten peaks starting from the Langdale valley. Includes Scafell Pike and involves 6,000 feet of ascent. Badge and certificate available for completions.

PENNINGTON ROUND

26 miles
A circuit of the Furness area including the summit of Hoad Hill. Moderate walking and varied terrain. Send SAE for route description to Brian Richmond, 31 Dartmouth Street, Barrow-in-Furness, Cumbria LA14 3AS.

SHAP STROLL

20 miles
Trans-Pennine Publications
A circuit from Shap which explores the far eastern area of the Lakes including Keld, Mosedale Head, Long Sleddale, Gatescarth Pass and Mardale.
Leaflet, certificate and badge for sale, send SAE with enquiries to Trans-Pennine Publications, Sunnybank, Drawbriggs Lane, Appleby-in-Westmorland, Cumbria CA16 6HY.

IN SEARCH OF WESTMORLAND

171 miles
Charles Emett, Cicerone Press
A demanding route following the boundary of the old county of Westmorland.
Includes the East Lakes fells and the high Pennine areas of Wild Boar Fell and Cross Fell.

WALKING THROUGH
THE LAKE DISTRICT
Michael Dunn, David and Charles, 1987
A book describing the routes of seven generally demanding walks.
Lakeland Horseshoe 88 miles
A high-level route taking in all four Lakeland threethousanders and other major fells in a week.
Back O'Skidda 29 miles
A high-level circuit of the Northern Lakes in three stages starting from Mungrisedale.
The Roman Way 53 miles
A five day linear walk linking together the Roman forts of Brocavum, Galava, Mediobogdum and Glannaventa.
The North-West Fells 24 miles
An introduction to the delights of the Lakeland mountains and ridges in a two day outing from Keswick.
The Valley Route 35 miles
A lower level walk from Eskdale to Patterdale via Wasdale Head, Rosthwaite and Grasmere in four sections.
The Hidden Valleys 15 miles
A one day round from Kentmere visiting Longsledale, Haweswater and Harter fell.
Heart Of Lakeland 33 miles
A three day high-level circuit including Crinkle Crags, Bowfell, Great Gable , Honister Pass, Glaramara and the Langdale Pikes.

WALKING TOUR OF LAKELAND

104 miles
Paul Buttle, Amadorn, 1997
A recently published route describing a seven day round of the Lakes starting at Staveley and finishing at Ambleside. Strenuous with over 26,000 feet of ascent. Lower-level options available.
Postal enquiries to: 18 Brewery Lane, Keswick, Cumbria CA12 5LJ.

LDWA HANDBOOK, A&C Black

The 1995 edition of the Long Distance Walkers' Handbook lists the routes below as anytime challenge walks. Information sheets are available from the addresses shown below. A new edition of the handbook is due for publication in 1998.

Lost Lancs Way 50 miles
A walk along the old Lancashire boundary north of the sands and now part of Cumbria.

That's Lyth 25 miles
A walk along the fringe of the Lakes taking in the limestone scenery of Cunswick Scar, Scout Scar and Whitbarow Scar.

Copies of both routes are available by sending 9"x6" SAE to Mr Frank Hodson, Toll Bar Cottage, Underbarrow, Kendal, Cumbria, LA8 8HB

Ullswater Circuit 46 miles
An extended circuit of Ullswater involving 8,000 feet of ascent. Certificate available.
Send SAE to Mr Paul Miler, 25 St Hugh's Close, Birkenhead, Merseyside, L43 4YS.

FOUR PASSES WALK

20 miles 4,500 feet
This route has been walked for nearly a century and is now regarded as something of a classic, although rarely mentioned in guidebooks. The YHA have organised a walk round it in recent years but it can, of course, be completed at any time. Their route based on Longthwaite Hostel, Borrowdale is as follows:
Styhead pass to Wasdale - Black Sail pass into Ennerdale - over Scarth Gap to Buttermere Lake - over Honister Hause by way of Warnscale and Drumhouse to avoid the Road. The old Honister Quarry track brings you back to Longthwaite through Johnny's Wood.

Lakeland Trails *update*

In order to keep you up-to- date with any amendments to the routes or guides listed in this book a news sheet will be published from January, 1999 to December, 2001 .

The news sheet will:

- advise of any new routes or mountain challenges
- list any changes to addresses and other amendments
- keep you up-to-date on the Lakeland Heritage routes - a list of recorded completions and the amounts donated to charity.

Send cheque for £1-00 payable to *Lakeland Heritage* plus SAE to:
Mountain Dawn Publications
10 Beaufort Grove,
Bradford
BD2 4L J

The full pound will be donated to Christian Aid and Amnesty International.

Forest Trails

There are nine forests in the Lakes area which provide for the recreational needs of visitors. All have paths suitable for walkers.

Whinlatter Forest Park GR 208 245
The main visitor centre for the North Lakes offering a variety of waymarked routes and a trail-orienteering course. Toilet, tea room and shop facilities. Guide maps and information available. Tel: (017687) 78469

Dodd Wood GR 234 283
Waymarked trails from car park with picnic areas, cafe and toilets- open April to October. Guide map from the Old Sawmill tearoom and Whinlatter Visitor Centre

Ennerdale GR 110 153
Scenic forest walks on waymarked trails from Bowness Knott car park , toilets and picnic area. Nine Becks Walk 10 miles, Liza Path 9 miles and Round The Lake 7 miles
Guide Map available from Whinlatter Visitor Centre

Setmurthy Forest GR 160 320
A developing woodland near Cockermouth with views over the Derwent Valley. Forest walks and orienteering course. Maps available from Cockermouth Leisure Centre Tel (01900) 823596

Grizedale Forest Park GR 335 945
The visitor centre for the southern Lakes with an extensive range of facilities including forest shop, adventure playground, picnic areas, exhibition, forest tearoom and waymarked trails including The Silurian Way and Sculpture Trails. Guide Maps available.
Tel: (01229) 860010

Other forests are located at **Miterdale,** close to the village of Eskdale Green; **Blengdale,** a small forest near the village of Gosforth; **Hardknott Forest** in the Duddon valley; and **Broughton Moor** a secluded forest south-east of Coniston.

Limited Mobility Trails

The Lake District National Park has produced a comprehensive guide to 21 locations where it is suitable to use wheelchairs. Routes vary from 0.5 to 8 miles in length and explore a varied selection of Lakeland landscapes.

Friars Crag, Keswick GR 265 229
The Bowderstone GR 254 168
Cat Bells Terrace GR 249 197
Keswick Railway GR 299 247
Braithwaite GR 228 236
Whinlatter Forest Park GR 207 245
Mungrisedale GR 365 301
Maggie's Bridge, Loweswater GR 135 210
Red Nab, Windermere GR 385 995
Bowness GR 399 963
Windermere GR 388 956
Grasmere riverside GR 337 076
Easedale, Grasmere GR 337 076
White Moss, Rydal GR 348064
Kentmere GR 455 041
Staveley, Kendal GR 470 987
Whitherslack GR 430 842
Tarn Hows GR 330 996
Monk Coniston GR 316 978
Grizedale Forest Park GR 336 944
Blea Tarn, Little Langdale GR 296 043

Countryside Access for People with Limited Mobility, Lake District National Park Office - available from National Park Information Centres on page 80

Nature and Town Trails

There are numerous trails throughout Cumbria, many suitable for wheelchairs. Enquire at the Information Centres on page 80 for individual locations and leaflets.

This section lists those routes which link the Lake District with other areas.

WAINWRIGHT'S COAST TO COAST

190 miles
Start St Bees Head, Cumbria
Finish Robin Hood's Bay, North Yorkshire
Ascent 16,000 feet
Maps Outdoor Leisure Maps 33 and 34
Coast to Coast Walk - St Bees Head to Keld,
Keld to Robin Hood's Bay.
A Coast to Coast Walk, Alfred Wainwright, originally published by Westmorland Gazette. 1973- now published by Michael Joseph with revisions
Wainwright's Coast to Coast Walk with photographs by Derry Brabbs, Michael Joseph, 1987.

A now classic journey from the Irish Sea to the North Sea devised by Alfred Wainwright and published in 1972. His object was to inspire walkers to take out the map and pioneer their own routes rather than following in the footsteps of officialdom. The 190 mile route links St Bees Head, south of Whitehaven, with Robin Hood's Bay, near Whitby; passes through the Lake District, Yorkshire Dales and North York Moors National Parks; uses rights of way and goes over high ground where possible. Perhaps the finest trail in England.

OTHER COAST TO COAST ROUTES

An Alternative Coast to Coast: Walney Island to Holy Island
192 miles
Denis Brook & Phil Hinchcliffe, Cicerone Press,1996

Lakeland To Lindisfarne
175 miles
Ravenglass to Holy Island
John Gillam, Crowood Press, 1995

North of England Way
320 km
Ravenglass to Scarborough
On Foot from Coast to Coast, The North of England Way, David Maughan, Penguin Books Ltd., 1997

The Ravenber
209 miles
Ravenglass to Berwick-upon-Tweed
The Ravenber, Ron Scholes, The Pentland Press, 1997

... and men go forth, and admire lofty mountains and broad seas, and raging torrents, and the ocean, and the course of stars, and forget themselves.

St Augustine, 4th Century

DALES WAY

81 miles- Ilkley to Bowness-on-Windermere
The Dales Way, Colin Speakman, Dalesman.1970.
A gentle walk through the heart of the Yorkshire Dales reaching a maximum height of 1,700 feet at Cam Head where it crosses the Pennine Way. Fascinating links from Leeds, Bradford and Harrogate make it possible for urban dwellers to literally step out of their doors and walk to the shores of Windermere.

LANCASHIRE TO LAKELAND

70 miles - Preston to Windermere.
The Lancashire-Lakeland Link, Jack Jowett, Owl Books, 1994.

A leisurely stroll with numerous variations, devised with the retired walker in mind.

LANCASTER CANAL

27 miles - Lancaster to Kendal
The Lancaster Canal, South Lakeland District Council. Free leaflet from Kendal and Kirkby Lonsdale Tourist Information Centres.
This towpath walk explores the history and wildlife of the canal. A Lancaster Canal Trust was founded in 1963 to help restore the full 53 miles to its former glory.

LIMESTONE LINK

13 miles - Arnside to Kirkby Lonsdale.
The Limestone Link ,South Lakeland District Council. Free leaflet available from Kirkby Lonsdale or Kendal Tourist Information Centres.
A waymarked walk through the limestone country of South Cumbria exploring the unique flora of limestone pavements and the history of the area.

THIRLMERE WAY

130 miles - Manchester to Thirlmere Dam.
Tim Cappelli, Sigma Leisure, 1992.
A walk along the route of Manchester's one hundred year-old water supply describing its history and geography. The aqueduct was designed to carry water from Thirlmere at a height of 590 feet above sea-level to Manchester at a height of 360 feet so the water would simply run downhill all the way. Its construction was not quite so simple; it took seven years and claimed numerous lives. The tunnel through Dunmail Raise took four years to complete and is one of the many tunnels throughout its 95 mile length. The route follows the course of the 7 feet diameter aqueduct and its Victorian engineers as closely as possible but detours to include other features of interest.

Thirlmere

PEAKS LAKES & ROUNDS

A Guide To

THE BOB GRAHAM ROUND

THE WAINWRIGHTS

THE LAKES TWO-THOUSANDS

MOUNTAIN CHALLENGES

CLASSIC ROUNDS

PEAKS LAKES & ROUNDS

THE ROUTE OF THE BOB GRAHAM ROUND

72 miles - 27,000 feet

STAGE ONE
Keswick to Threlkeld

1 Skiddaw
2 Great Calva
3 Blencathra

STAGE TWO
Threlkeld to Dunmail

4 Clough Head
5 Great Dodd
6 Watson's Dodd
7 Stybarrow Dodd
8 Raise
9 White Side
10 Helvellyn Lower Man
11 Helvellyn
12 Nethermost
13 Dollywaggon Pike
14 Fairfield
15 Seat Sandal

STAGE FIVE
Honister Pass to Keswick

40 Dale Head
41 Hindscarth
42 Robinson

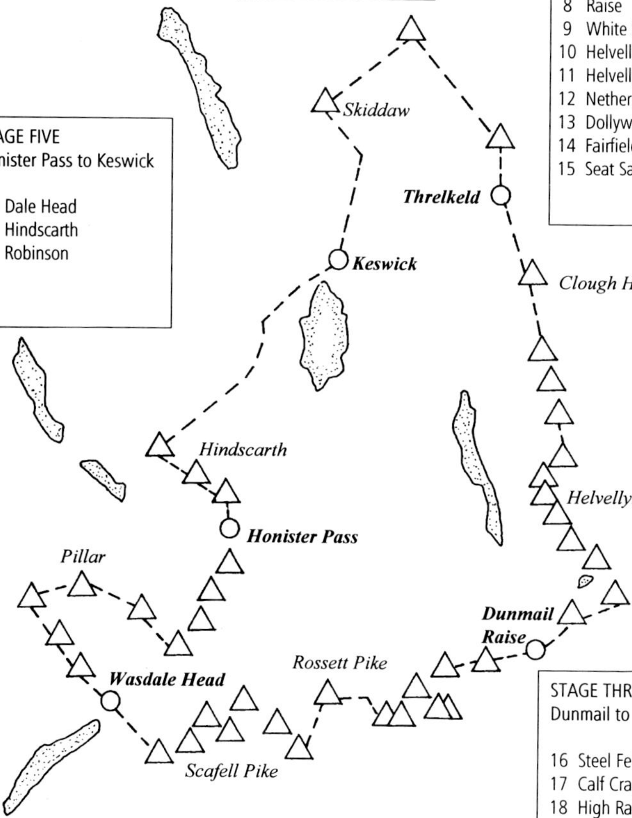

STAGE THREE
Dunmail to Wasdale

16 Steel Fell
17 Calf Crag
18 High Raise
19 Sergeant Man
20 Thunacar Knott
21 Harrison Stickle
22 Pike O'Stickle
23 Rossett Pike
24 Bowfell
25 Esk Pike
26 Great End
27 Ill Crag
28 Broad Crag
29 Scafell Pike
30 Scafell

STAGE FOUR
Wasdale to Honister Pass

31 Yewbarrow
32 Red Pike
33 Steeple
34 Pillar
35 Kirk Fell
36 Great Gable
37 Green Gable
38 Brandreth
39 Grey Knotts

Fell running is part of the great sporting tradition of the Lake District and one of its finest institutions is the Bob Graham Club. The Round was inaugurated by Bob Graham of Keswick when setting a new 24 hour fellwalking record. Fred Rogerson and A.H.Griffin founded the club in 1971 in response to an increasing interest in long-distance fellrunning. To become a member of the club Graham's round of 42 peaks has to be completed in 24 hours. This involves some 72 miles of mountain terrain and 27,000 feet of ascent. Although membership has now reached over one thousand the annual completion rate has rarely exceeded fifty percent throughout the history of the club. It has become the benchmark of all peak-bagging runs and has spawned similar mountain challenges throughout England, Scotland and Wales. The round itself has its origins in the Lake District fell walking record. As early as 1903 W T Palmer in his book **Lakeland Dells and Fells** donates a chapter to charting progress of the record. He starts in the 1860's by crediting the Reverend J M Elliot with a round of ten peaks involving some 6,500 feet of ascent and 15 miles. A succession of other walks extended the record when in 1901 Henry Broadrick and Cecil Dawson, a legendary figure famous for his Peakland bogtrotting, set a record of 67 miles and 16,600 feet. Other notable record holders included Dr A W Wakefield, who was involved on the 1922 Everest attempt and Eustace Thomas, known for his exploits in the Peak District with the Rucksack Club. Wakefield completed a route of 70 miles, 22 peaks and 23,500 feet in 22 hours 7 minutes which Thomas improved on and later extended at the age of 54.

Bob Graham made his first attempt on the record in 1931 but was not successful until the following year at the age of 42 when he completed 42 peaks. The number of peaks was selected to correspond with his age. His record stood for the next 28 years. The 1960's saw a revived interest in the record when Harry Griffin of the Lancashire Evening Post threw down the gauntlet of a real challenge amid the publicity given to Dr Barbara Moore's Lands End to John O'Groats walk. Alan and Ken Heaton responded. First Alan broke the record with a round of 22 hours 18 minutes which Ken later extended to a route of 51 peaks in 22 hours 13 minutes. A succession of records followed including 56 peaks by Eric Beard, 60 by Alan Heaton, 72 peaks by Joss Naylor in 1975, 76 by Mark McDermott in 1988 and finally 77 in 1997 by Mark Hartnell.

JUST FOR THE RECORD

24 HOUR RECORDS

- ☐ Mark Hartnell : 77 Peaks and 40,000 feet of ascent in 23 hours 26 minutes (1997)
- ☐ Anne Stentiford : 62 Peaks in 23 hours 17 minutes (1994)

BOB GRAHAM RECORDS

- ☐ Billy Bland : 13 hours 54 minutes (1982)
- ☐ Anne Stentiford : 18 hours 49 minutes (1991)
- ☐ Club Members January 1998 = 1062
- ☐ Mike Hartley completed a 23 hours 48 minutes Bob Graham Round after completing the Scottish Ramsey Round of 24 Munros and 28,000 feet in 21 hours 14 minutes. This was followed by the Welsh Paddy Buckley Round of 47 Peaks and 28,000 feet giving a total running time for all three consecutive rounds of 3 days 14 hours 10 minutes.

FURTHER INFORMATION

42 PEAKS The Story of The Bob Graham Club - available from Lakes bookshops.

REGISTRATION

All attempts should be registered in advance with Fred Rogerson, the Chairman. Send SAE for details to : Fred Rogerson, Tethers End, Lindeth, Windermere, Cumbria LA23 3NH.

THE WAINWRIGHTS

Peaks Lakes & Rounds

The fleeting hours of life of those who love the hills is quickly spent, but the hills are eternal. Always there will be the lonely ridge, the dancing beck, the silent forest; always there will be the exhilaration of the summits. These are for the seeking, and those who seek and find while there is yet time will be blessed in mind and body.

Alfred Wainwright , 1965

It took Alfred Wainwright eleven years from 1954 to 1965 to climb, explore and chart the 214 summits which he meticulously illustrated in his seven pictorial guides to the Lake District. Since that time they have provided both the means and the inspiration by which generations of walkers have come to know the Lakeland fells. As more people have taken to the hills Wainwright bagging has grown in popularity and provides a local version of Scottish Munro bagging. Apart from being more accessible, the Wainwrights provide a pleasant and contrasting mixture of high and low fells. This means that even on the foulest Lakeland day when the high tops are being battered by rain, wind or snow, a more modest ascent of a humbler fell may be possible.

Completions of all the Wainwrights have been recorded since the early 1970's. Then, in the eighties, the idea caught the imagination of a number of long distance fell runners. Forty years old Chris Bland of Stonethwaite was the first to attempt a seven books in seven days run in 1981. As this was to raise money for the Borrowdale Church Restoration Fund he decided to start and finish each day at a church. He fell short of the 214 summits by just 22 but established that the feat would be achievable in better weather conditions.

Long distance mountain runner Alan Heaton was the next to have a go but on a revised route starting and finishing at the Moot Hall Keswick. The 57 year old veteran completed all the tops in 9 days 16 hours 42 minutes. He was partially delayed by a visit to Keswick hospital with a toe injury, which nearly aborted the run.

The following year Joss Naylor attempted the round to celebrate his 50th year and raise funds for the Arthritis Research Council. He set a new record of 7 days, 1 hour and 25 minutes. The distance was approximately 391 miles involving 121,000 feet of ascent. An account of the run together with his schedule has been published in a handy booklet called **Joss Naylor MBE Was Here** which is still available from some Lakes outdoor shops.

A more recent and less arduous challenge was completed by Geoff Saunders of St Helens to celebrate his sixtieth birthday in 1995. This consisted of a 60 mile route linking together the highest Wainwright in each book to create a **Seven Summits Walk.** For those who intend to take a little longer to systematically bag all the Wainwrights, there is now a small industry of merchandise in addition to the seven pictorial guides. These include logbooks, Wainwright maps and a wall chart of the Wainwright fells as well as a range of Wainwright outdoor gear including, of course, a teeshirt. For anyone wishing to register their achievement a Hillwalkers' Register is maintained by Alan Castle,details below. When the seven books of 214 summits have been completed there are always the 102 outlying fells!

Further Information

- ☐ Pictorial Guide to the Lakeland Fells Books one to seven, 1955-1966, now published by Michael Joseph.
- ☐ The Outlying Fells of Lakeland,1974
- ☐ The Walker's Logbook, Volumes one and two, Michael Joseph, 1993
- ☐ Wainwright The Biography, Hunter Davies, Michael Joseph 1995
- ☐ The Wainwrights - A wallchart of the Lakeland fells, Kevin Borman, 1989
- ☐ Joss Naylor MBE Was Here, Joss Naylor, Klets, 1987

Hillwalkers' Register

For details send SAE and two 1st class stamps to : Alan Castle, Glebe House, Ravenstone, Buckinghamshire MK46 5AR

Eastern Fells

Fell	Height
Arnison Crag	1424
Birkhouse Moor	2350
Birks	2040
Catsycam	2917
Clough Head	2381
Dollywagon Pike	2810
Dove Crag	2603
Fairfield	2863
Glenridding Dodd	1425
Gowbarrow Fell	1579
Great Dodd	2807
Great Mell Fell	1760
Great Rigg	2513
Hart Crag	2698
Hart Side	2481
Hartsop above How	1870
Helvellyn	3118
Heron Pike	2003
High Hartsop Dodd	1702
High Pike	2155
Little Hart Crag	2091
Little Mell Fell	1657
Low Pike	1657
Middle Dodd	2106
Nab Scar	1450
Nethermost Pike	2920
Raise	2889
Red Screes	2541
Saint Sunday Crag	2756
Seat Sandal	2415
Sheffield Pike	2232
Stone Arthur	1652
Stybarrow Dodd	2770
Watson's Dodd	2584
Whiteside	2832

Far Eastern Fells

Fell	Height
Angletarn Pikes	1857
Arthur's Pike	1747
Beda Fell	1664
Bonscale Pike	1718
Branstree	2333
Brock Crags	1842
Caudale Moor	2502
Froswick	2359

Far Eastern Fells

Continued

Fell	Height
Gray Crag	2286
Grey Crag	2093
Hallin Fell	1271
Harter Fell	2539
Hartsop Dodd	2018
High Raise	2634
High Street	2718
Ill Bell	2476
Kentmere Pike	2397
Kidsty Pike	2560
The Knott	2423
Loadpot Hill	2201
Mardale Ill Bell	2496
The Nab	1887
Place Fell	2154
Rampsgill Hill	2581
Rest Dodd	2278
Sallows	1691
Selside Pike	2142
Shipman Knotts	1926
Sour Howes	1568
Steel Knotts	1414
Tarn Crag	2176
Thornthwaite Crag	2569
Troutbeck Tongue	1191
Wansfell	1597
Wether Hill	2210
Yoke	2309

Central Fells

Fell	Height
Armbroth Fell	1570
Bleaberry Fell	1932
Blea Rigg	1776
Calf Crag	1762
Eagle Crag	1650
Gibson Knott	1379
Grange Fell	1363
Great Crag	1500
Harrison Stickle	2403
Helm Crag	1299
High Raise	2500
High Rigg	1163
High Seat	1995
High Tove	1665
Loft Crag	2270

Central Fells

Continued

Fell	Height
Loughrigg Fell	1001
Pavey Ark	2288
Pike o'Stickle	2323
Raven Crag	1520
Sergeant Man	2414
Sergeant Crag	1873
Silver How	1292
Steel Fell	1811
Tarn Crag	1801
Thunacar Knott	2351
Ullscarf	2370
Walla Crag	1234

Southern Fells

Fell	Height
Allen Crags	2572
Black Fell	1056
Bowfell	2960
Brimfell	2611
Cold Pike	2259
Coniston Old Man	2633
Crinkle Crags	2816
Dow Crag	2555
Esk Pike	2903
Glaramara	2560
Great Carrs	2575
Great End	2984
Green Crag	1602
Grey Friar	2536
Hard Knott	1803
Harter Fell	2140
Holme Fell	1040
Illgill Head	1983
Lingmell	2649
Lingmoor	1530
Pike o' Blisco	2304
Rossett Pike	2106
Rosthwaite Fell	1807
Scafell	3162
Scafell Pike	3210
Seathwaite Fell	1970
Slight Side	2499
Swirl Howe	2630
Wetherlam	2502
Whin Rigg	1755

THE WAINWRIGHTS

Northern Fells

Bakestall	2189
Bannerdale Crags	2230
Binsey	1466
Blencathra	2847
Bowscale Fell	2306
Brae Fell	1920
Carl Side	2420
Carrock Fell	2174
Dodd	1612
Great Calva	2265
Great Cockup	1720
Great Sca Fell	2131
High Pike	2157
Knott	2329
Latrigg	1203
Longlands Fell	1580
Long Side	2405
Lonsdale Fell	2344
Meal Fell	1770
Mungrisdale Common	2068
Skiddaw	3053
Skiddaw Little Man	2837
Souther Fell	1680
Ullcock Pike	2230

North Western Fells

Ard Crags	1860
Barf	1536
Barrow	1494
Broom Fell	1670
Castle Crag	985
Catbells	1481
Causey Pike	2035
Dale Head	2473
Eel Crag	2749
Grasmoor	2791
Graystones	1476
Grisedale Pike	2593
High Spy	2143
Hindscarth	2385
Hopegill Head	2525
Knott Rigg	1790

North Western Fells

Continued

Ling Fell	1224
Lord's Seat	1811
Maiden Moor	1887
Outerside	1863
Rannerdale Knotts	1160
Robinson	2417
Sail	2530
Sale Fell	1170
Scar Crags	2205
Wandhope	2533
Whinlatter	1696
Whiteless Pike	2159
Whiteside	2317

Western Fells

Base Brown	2120
Blake Fell	1878
Brandreth	2344
Buckbarrow	1410
Burnbank Fell	1580
Caw Fell	2288
Crag Fell	1710
Fellbarrow	1363
Fleetwith Pike	2126
Gavel Fell	1720
Great Bourne	2019
Great Gable	2949
Green Gable	2603
Grey Knotts	2287
Grike	1596
Haycock	2618
Haystacks	1900
Hen Comb	1661
High Crag	2443
High Stile	2644
Kirk Fell	2630
Lank Rigg	1775
Low Fell	1360
Mellbreak	1676
Middle Fell	1908
Pillar	2927
Red Pike (Buttermere)	2479

Western Fells

Continued

Red Pike (Wasdale)	2707
Scoat Fell	2760
Seatallan	2266
Startling Dodd	2085
Steeple	2687
Yewbarrow	2058

The height shown for each summit is that given by Wainwright; this may differ with current maps and other sources.

Summits in each book

Eastern Fells 35
Far Eastern 36
Central Fells 27
Southern Fells 30
Northern Fells 24
North Western Fells 29
Western Fells 33

Total of 214 summits

Highest Summits in each of the above books

Helvellyn 3117
High Street 2717
High Raise 2500
Scafell Pike 3209
Skiddaw 3054
Crag Hill 2753
Great Gable 2949

To those who prefer the dull routine of well remembered ascents, the peak-bagger is one who dashes soullessly from top to top and whose memory of the day can be summed up in a tick on a list. But to me collecting tops in a list provides the framework for widening experiences in the fascination of fresh country, unknown hills, and other natural beauties. The pursuit of two-thousands has taken me to many places I should otherwise never have visited; it has, in fact taken me into some of the most God-forsaken spots in this country as well as to some of the most delectable.

Edward Moss, 1952

Moss completed all the two-thousands in 1951.

The two-thousand foot contour is widely accepted as the level at which a hill graduates into a mountain. While there is general agreement on the height, there have been various definitions as to what constitutes a separate and different mountain. For those who simply want a framework for systematically visiting all the mountains in the Lake District the list of 127 Wainwrights that exceed 2,000 feet is adequate, although it would probably be worth checking on recent maps to see if any of his summits of 1950 feet or more have now been promoted to mountain status. Reference can also be made to A.H.Griffin's **Freeman of the Hills** which was dedicated to the modest challenge of visiting them all at the age of sixty-seven!

Anyone who has ambitions of becoming a more dedicated peak bagger and ultimately covering the whole of England and Wales may wish to use one of the national lists. Sir Hugh Munro's tables of Scottish mountains exceeding 3,000 feet published in 1891 no doubt inspired a number of mountaineering club members to pioneer lists of two-thousands and twenty-fives south of the border. Among these were names such as Corbett, Simpson, Elmsie, and Doherty whose work was published privately or in club journals. It was only in 1973 that George Bridge revisited the task and later made his work available to the general public.

More recently there has been a spate of guide-books to the Lakeland summits as well as national lists of summits. Among these John and Anne Nuttall's two volumes of the Mountains of England and Wales stand out and have been widely adopted by serious peak baggers. Their definition of a separate mountain is one which is 2,000 feet and rises above the surrounding land by at least 50 feet on all sides. Heights are based on the latest survey information and each summit has a comprehensive route description. Their list of Lakeland summits totals 170. A chart locating all the 251 English and 181 Welsh Nuttall summits is now published by Harvey Maps. Alan Castle maintains a register of completions of anyone who completes all the national two-thousands, details are given below.

A natural subdivision of the Lakeland two-thousands is those summits over two-thousand five hundred feet in elevation. There are 67 which fit the Nuttall definition while Wainwright lists 57 of his fells as being above the mark. These numbers have become within the grasp of long distance fell runners like Joss Naylor. In 1996 he celebrated his sixty years with a traverse of 60 summits in some 36 hours.

Further Information

The Mountains of England and Wales, George Bridge, West Col Publications, 1973

Freeman of the Hills, A.H.Griffin, Robert Hale Limited, 1978

The Mountains of England and Wales volume 2 , John and Anne Nuttall, Cicerone Press, 1990

Mountain Chart of England and Wales, Harvey Map Sevices Ltd, 1996

Hillwalkers' Register

Send SAE and two first class stamps to Alan Castle, Recorder, Hillwalkers' Register, Glebe House, Ravenstone, Buckinghamshire, MK46 5AR

LAKES FOUR THREE-THOUSANDS

Start and Finish Keswick
Distance 45 miles
Maps Outdoor Leisure The English Lakes - North West, South West, North East
Ascent 10,500 feet

There are are only four peaks in England which surpass the height of 3000 feet - Scafell Pike, 3,209 ft, Scafell, 3,163 ft, Helvellyn, 3,117 ft and Skiddaw 3,054 ft. To ascend them in one continuous outing has become an increasingly popular challenge. As early as 1870 a similar route had inspired two walkers named Watson and Wilson. Starting from Keswick they are recorded as having completed a 48 mile round, excluding Scafell, in under 21 hours. No mean achievement in an age of no torches, lightweight gear or well-worn paths! Since 1965 the Ramblers Association have organised an annual event each June. It starts at 2 am from Keswick Rugby Club and has a 22 hours limit. Details of the Four Peaks Challenge walk are available from January each year. Send SAE to, Vicki Farrar, Springfield, Ravenglass, Cumbria CA18 1SW.

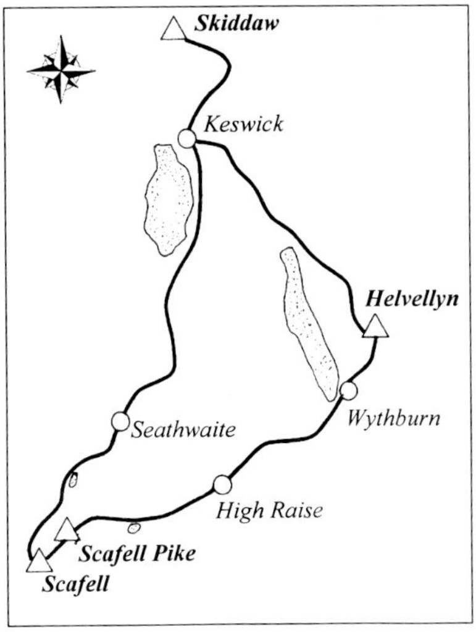

THREE OLD COUNTY SUMMITS

Start and Finish Grasmere
Distance 35 miles
Maps Outdoor Leisure The English Lakes - South East, North East, North West
Ascent 9,000 feet

Prior to 1974 the Lake District was divided between Westmorland, Cumberland and Lancashire and this walk visited the highest points in each of those ancient counties. Today Cumbria embraces all three summits and has even laid claim to some of the finest fells in the Pennines. Leaving out Skiddaw and Scafell it perhaps makes a more satisfying route than four threethousanders as it crosses few roads and maintains high ground throughout. Between Scafell Pike and The Old Man there is the option of the high level route over Crinkle Crags to the Three Shire Stone or the valley route to Cockley Beck.

An annual fell race for teams of two is held each June. Details are contained in the fixtures calendar of the Fell Runners Association. See page 84 for details.

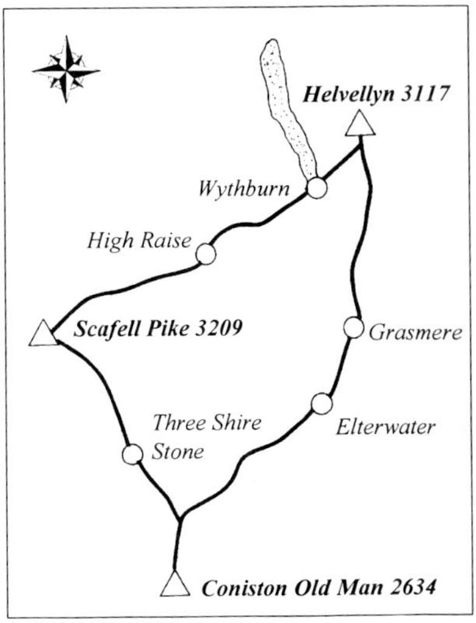

For those not exhausted by the prospect of the Four three-thousands or Old County Tops here is a brief outline of some other recent notable mountain challenges.

Lakeland's Ten Highest Peaks
A linear route starting from Burnthwaite Farm, Wasdale to the top of Skiddaw. Includes Great Gable, Scafell, Scafell Pike, Broad Crag, Ill Crag, Great End, Bowfell, Helvellyn, Skiddaw Little Man. Joss Naylor set a record of 6 hrs 56 mins in 1975.

Lakes and Meres
This visits the 26 major lakes and tarns in a route of some 105 miles and 17,000 feet of ascent. Loweswater, Crummock Water, Buttermere, Ennerdale, Waswater, Devoke Water, Goats Water, Low Water, Levers Water, Coniston Water, Esthwaite Water, Elterwater, Grasmere, Rydal Water, Windermere, Kentmere, Skeggles Water, Haweswater, Small Water, Blea Water, Hayeswater, Brotherswater, Ullswater, Thirlmere , Derwentwater to Overwater.
A record of 17 hrs 14 mins was set by Joss Naylor in 1983.

Lakes 2,500's
A traverse of 71 tops, 42,000 feet and 105 miles was first completed by the Rucksack Club in 1968. Since then there have been several variations including a circuit of 61 tops and 116 miles by Steve Parr in 1984 and more recently, in 1996, Joss Naylor's 60 peaks at 60 in aid of Multiple Sclerosis Research. This route, based on the Wainwrights, started on the Walna Scar road and finished in Glenridding some 40,000 feet and 105 miles later.

Leeds Town Hall to Scafell Pike
The longest ascent of Scafell ever made - 120 miles via Whernside, the highest point in Yorkshire. Instigated by the West Yorkshire Group of the Long Distance Walkers' Association to celebrate their tenth birthday.

JOSS NAYLOR'S LAKELAND CHALLENGE
This 48 mile challenge with 16,000 feet of ascent is aimed at the over 50 age group to help raise money for charity. A limited number of inscribed tankards donated by Chris Brasher are available for successful completions provided at least £100 is raised for any chosen charity.

The Challenge
Over 50's - 12hours (14 hours - women)
Over 60's - 18 hours
Over 65's - 24 hours

The Route
Leg one Start: Roehead GR 477 237
Barton Fell, Arthur Pike, Loadpot Hill,Wether Hill, Red Crag, Raven Howe, High Raise, Kidsty Pike, Rampsgill Head, High Street, Thornthwaite Beacon, Stoney Cove Pike, Pike How, Kirkstone Pass.
Leg two Red Screes, Hart Crag, Fairfield, Seat Sandal, Dunmail Raise.
Leg three Steel Fell, High Raise, Rossett Pike, Bowfell, Esk Pike, Great End, Great Gable, Kirkfell, Pillar, Scoat Fell, Steeple, Haycock, Seatallan, Middle Fell.
Finish: Greendale Bridge GR 143 056

Send SAE for details to Monica Shone, 21 Woburn Drive, Hale, Altrincham, Cheshire, WA15 8LZ

Shap to Ravenglass
A 42 mile classic east- west traverse via Swindale, High Street, Patterdale, Grisedale Tarn, Dunmail Raise, Steel Fell, High Raise, Angle Tarn, Bow Fell and Eskdale.

Further Information
Stud marks on the summits - A History of Amateur Fell Racing: 1861-1983, Bill Smith, SKG Publications 1985
Long Days in the Hills, A.H.Griffin, Robert Hale Limited, 1974
The Big Walks, Ken Wilson & Richard Gilbert, Diadem Books, 1980

One of the great characteristics of the Lake District is the lofty promenades that divide one valley from another. After an initial steep ascent the walker can enjoy a gentle roller-coaster ride round a skyline of summits before returning back to the valley bottom.
Many of these routes have been popular for decades and feature regularly in Lakeland walking guides while others have become the routes of annual fell races.

Further Information
The Big Walks, Ken Wilson and Richard Gilbert, Diadem Books, 1980
Wild Walks, Ken Wilson and Richard Gilbert, Diadem Books, 1988
Classic Walks, Ken Wilson and Richard Gilbert, Diadem Books, 1982
Fellwalking with Wainwright, Michael Joseph, 1984
Stud marks on the summits, Bill Smith, SKG Publications, 1985

Borrowdale Round

Distance - 17 miles
Ascent - 6,500 feet
Start - Rosthwaite GR 259 148
Map - Outdoor Leisure The English Lakes - North West

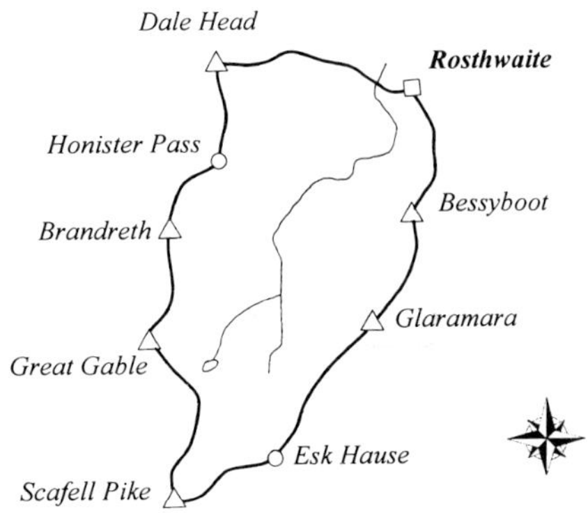

Buttermere Round

Distance - 13 miles
Ascent - 5,000 feet
Start - Buttermere GR 175 170
Map - Outdoor Leisure The English Lakes - North West

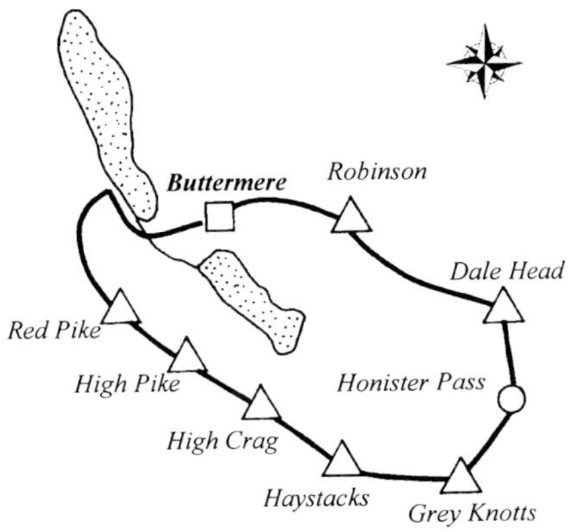

Fairfield Horseshoe

Distance - 9 miles
Ascent - 3,000 feet
Start - Rydal GR 365 062
Maps - Outdoor Leisure The Lake District - South East and North East

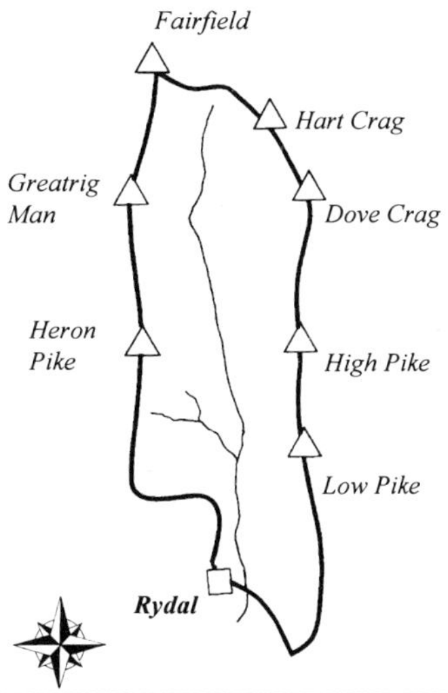

Kentmere Round

Distance - 12 miles
Ascent - 3,500 feet
Start - Kentmere GR 455 041
Map - Outdoor Leisure The Lake District - South East

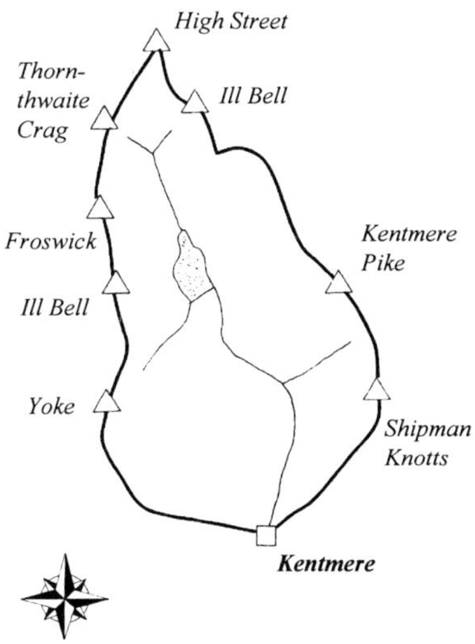

Ennerdale Horseshoe

Distance - 23 miles
Ascent - 8,000 feet
Start - Ennerdale Water car park GR 085 154
Map - Outdoor Leisure The English Lakes - North West

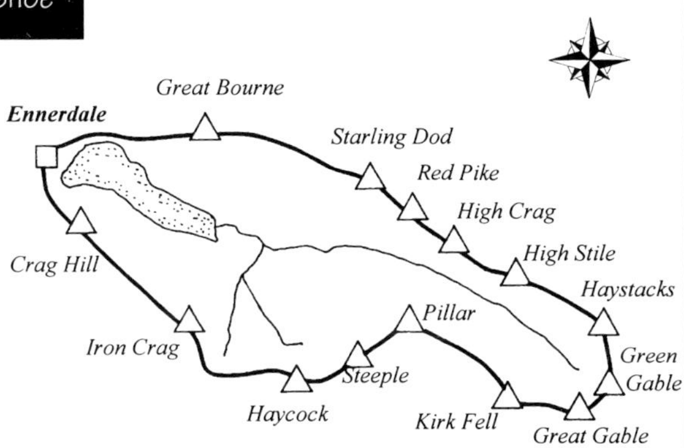

Coledale Round

Distance - 9 miles
Ascent - 3,500 feet
Start - Braithwaite GR 230 236
Maps - Outdoor Leisure The English Lakes - North West

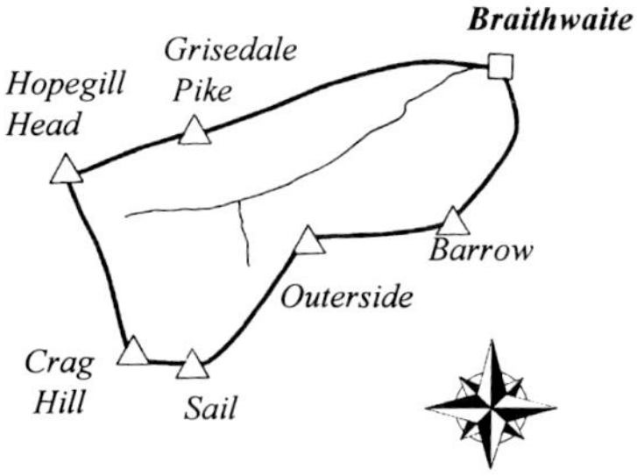

Newlands Round

Distance - 9 miles
Ascent - 3,500 feet
Start - Little Town GR 234 195
Maps - Outdoor Leisure The English Lakes - North West

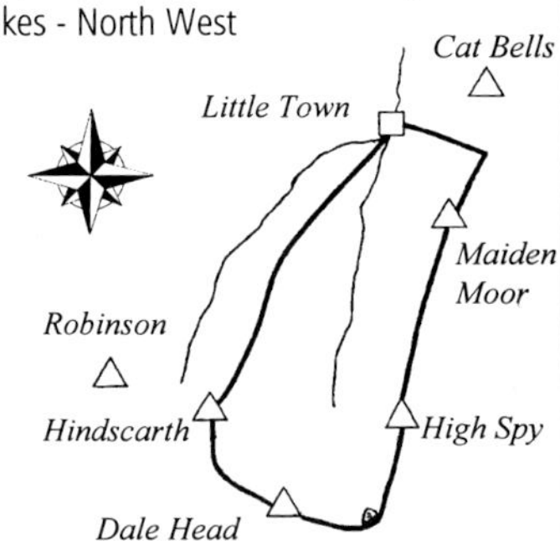

Langdale Circuit

Distance - 18 miles
Ascent - 5,000 feet
Start - Elterwater GR 328 047
Maps - Outdoor Leisure The English Lakes - South West

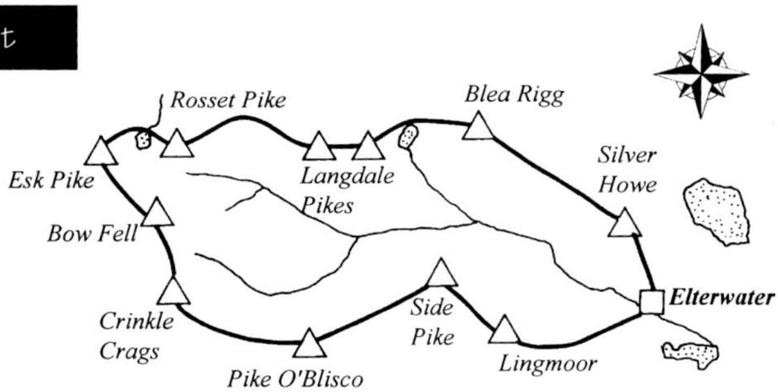

Mosedale Horseshoe and Wasdale Circuit

Wasdale Circuit - 21 miles, 9,000 ft
Start - Woodhow GR 140 042

Mosedale Horseshoe - 8 miles, 3,000 ft
Start - Wasdale Head GR 187 088

Map - Outdoor Leisure The English Lakes - South West

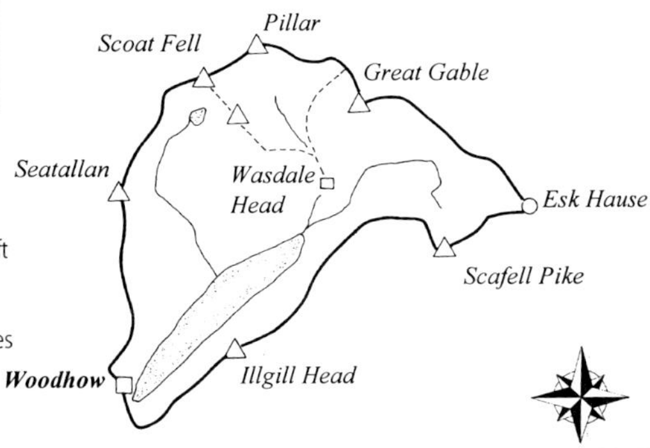

INFORMATION CENTRES

ACCOMMODATION

PUBLIC TRANSPORT

ORGANISATIONS

GENERAL INFORMATION

INFORMATION CENTRES

National Park & Tourist Information Centres

i

These information centres offer a full range of visitor services including:

- ☐ accommodation booking
- ☐ guidebooks and maps
- ☐ local transport information
- ☐ ideas of where to go and what to do
- ☐ special events
- ☐ local weather forecast

National Park Centres

BROCKHOLE VISITOR CENTRE
Windermere (on the A591)
Tel: (015394) 46601
This is the main visitor centre for the park. Exhibitions and gardens, gift and bookshop, restaurant and tearooms, plus a regular events programme.

CONISTON Ruskin Avenue
Tel: (015394) 41533

BOWNESS BAY Glebe Road
Tel: (015394) 42895

GRASMERE Red Bank Road
Tel: (015394) 35245

HAWKSHEAD Main Car Park
Tel: (015394) 36525

KESWICK Lake Road
Tel: (017687) 72803

POOLEY BRIDGE The Square
Tel: (017684) 86530

SEATOLLER BARN Borrowdale
Tel: (017687) 77294

ULLSWATER Main Car Park
Tel: (017684) 82414

Tourist Information Centres

AMBLESIDE
Church Street, Ambleside,
Cumbria CA9 3JB
Tel: (015394) 32582

APPLEBY
Moot Hall, Boroughgate,
Appleby -in-Westmorland,
Cumbria CA16 6XD
Tel: (017683) 51177

BARROW-IN-FURNESS
Forum 28, Duke Street,
Barrow-in-Furness,
Cumbria LA14 1HU
Tel: (01229) 870156

BRAMPTON
The Moot Hall, Market Place,
Brampton,
Cumbria CA8 8JH
Tel: (016977) 3433

CARLISLE
Carlisle Visitor Centre,
Carlisle,
Cumbria CA3 8JH
Tel: (01228) 512444

COCKERMOUTH
Town Hall, Cockermouth,
Cumbria CA13 9NP
Tel: (01900) 822634

EGREMONT
12 Main Street, Egremont
Cumbria CA22 2DW
Tel: (01946) 820693

GRANGE-OVER-SANDS
Victoria Hall, Main Street,
Grange-over-Sands
Cumbria LA11 6DP
Tel: (015395) 34026

KESWICK
Moot Hall, Market Square,
Keswick
Cumbria CA12 4JR
Tel: (017687) 72645

MARYPORT
Maryport Maritime Museum,
1 Senhouse Street,
Maryport,
Cumbria CA15 6AB
Tel: (01900) 813738

MILLOM
Millom Folk Museum,
St George's Road, Millom,
Cumbria LA18 4DQ
Tel: (01229) 772555

PENRITH
Middlegate, Penrith,
Cumbria CA11 7PT
Tel: (01768) 867466

RAVENGLASS
Ravenglass & Eskdale
Railway Station,
Ravenglass,
Cumbria CA18 1SW
Tel: (01229) 717278

SILLOTH-ON-SOLWAY
The Green, Silloth, Carlisle,
Cumbria CA5 4QP
Tel: (016973) 31944

ULVERSTON
Coronation Hall,
County Square, Ulverston,
LA12 7LZ
Tel: (01229) 587120

WHITEHAVEN
Market Hall, Market Place,
Whitehaven
Cumbria CA28 7JG
Tel: (01946) 695678

Bed & Breakfast

☐ The **Tourist Information Centres** listed on page 80 will be pleased to assist with accommodation requirements.

☐ The **Ramblers' Association** publish a **Yearbook and Accommodation Guide** each year which is available from national booksellers. It is also provided free as one of the benefits of membership - see page 84.

☐ A **Western Lakes & Coasts Accommodation Guide** is available from The Tourism Office, Copeland B.C., Whitehaven CA28 7SH
Tel (01946) 695678

Camping

Details of campsites are included in the national park publication **Caravan and Tent Guide** obtainable from the national park information centres listed on page 80.

Youth Hostels

The YHA provides an extensive network of hostels throughout the Lake District which are open to all age groups. You have to be a member but you can join on arrival. Accommodation is provided in comfortable bunk-bedded rooms with all bedding provided. These are usually in single sex dormitories although some hostels have rooms for families or couples. Most hostels provide meals as well as self catering kitchens and other facilities such as a drying room and communal areas. Prices vary according to the grade of hostel and whether you are an adult or under 18.
Send for details to:

YHA National Office,
8 St Stephen's Hill,
St Albans, Herts AL1 2DY

Youth Hostels - continued

Hostels in the Lake District are listed below showing the grid reference location and telephone number

AMBLESIDE GR 377 031
Tel: (015394) 32304

ARNSIDE GR 452 783
Tel: (01524) 761 781

BLACK SAIL GR 194 124
(Ennerdale) No phone

BORROWDALE GR 254 142
Tel: (017687) 77257

BUTTERMERE GR 178 168
Tel: (017687) 70245

CARLISLE GR 386 569
Tel: (01228) 23934

CARROCK FELL GR 358 355
Tel: (016974) 78325

COCKERMOUTH GR 118 298
Tel: (01900) 822561

CONISTON COPPERMINES
GR 289 986
Tel: (015394) 41261

CONISTON HOLLY HOW
GR 302 980
Tel: (015394) 41323

DERWENTWATER GR 268 200
Tel: (017687) 77246

ELTERWATER GR 327 046
Tel: (015394) 37245

ENNERDALE GR 142 141
Tel: (01946) 861237

ESKDALE GR 195 010
Tel: (019467) 23219

GRASMERE BUTTERLIP HOW
GR 336 077
Tel: (015394) 35316

GRASMERE THORNEY HOW
GR 332 084
Tel: (015394) 35591

HAWKSHEAD GR 354 966
Tel: (015394) 36293

HELVELLYN GR 366 173
Tel: (017684) 82269

HONISTER HAUSE GR 224 135
Tel: (017687) 77267

KENDAL GR 515 924
Tel: (01539) 724066

KESWICK GR 267 235
Tel: (017687) 72484

LANGDALE GR 338 052
Tel: (015394) 37313

PATTERDALE GR 339 156
Tel: (017684) 82394

SKIDDAW HOUSE GR 288 291
Tel: (016974) 78325
NO ACCESS BY CAR

TEBAY GR 618 045
Tel: (015396) 24286

THIRLMERE GR 318 190
Tel: (017687) 73224

WASTWATER GR 145 045
Tel: (019467) 262222

WINDERMERE GR 405 013
Tel: (015394) 43543

COAST to COAST WALK

The regional office offers a central booking service for all or part of the route. Contact:
YHA Northern England
Regional Office,
PO BOX 11,
Matlock,
Derbyshire,
DE4 2XA

i

Camping Barns

A camping barn is a stone barn providing simple overnight shelter so you do not have to carry a tent. They have a wooden sleeping platform, table, cooking bench, cold tap and WC plus a bucket, bowl, clothes hooks and waste bags. You will need to take a sleeping bag, foam mat, torch, cooking stove and warm clothes.

There is a network of eleven barns in the Lake District most of which will accommodate a dozen people.

Central Booking only - contact:
National Park Information Centre
31 Lake Road
Keswick
Cumbria CA12 5DQ
Tel: (017687) 72803

Catbells GR 243 208
Newlands valley

Eagle' s Nest GR 258 259
Near Keswick

Tarnflat GR 947 146
St Bees Head

Swirral GR 364 174
Below Helvellyn range

Mill House GR 080 044
Near the coast

Hudscales GR 331 375
Near Caldbeck

Swallow GR 116 226
Loweswater valley

Fell End GR 239 881
South western fells

Cragg GR 174 172
Near Buttermere

Dinah Hoggus GR 259 150
Near Rosthwaite

Blake Beck GR 367 278
Near Blencathra

Heritage Trail Accommodation

The accommodation list below is for information and assistance only and should not be taken as a specific recommendation. You should satisfy yourself that all accommodation meets your specific requirements before making a booking .

BED & BREAKFAST

Keswick
There is a plentiful supply of B & B in the area. Contact the local Tourist Information Centre - tel: (017687) 72645. Also the **Western Lakes & Coast Accommodation Guide** covers the area (see page 81).

Grange-in-Borrowdale

Mrs Judith Figg
Tel (017687) 77607
Grayrigg
Grange-in-Borrowdale
CUMBRIA CA12 5UQ

Mrs J Weir
Tel (017687) 77616
Pennybrigg
Grange-in-Borrowdale
CUMBRIA CA12 5UQ

Mrs Janet Hind
Tel (017687) 77674
Grange Fell
Grange-in-Borrowdale
CUMBRIA CA12 5UQ

Margaret & John Dormer
(017687) 77305
Castle Cragg Country Guest House
Grange-in-Borrowdale
CUMBRIA CA12 5UQ

Buttermere

Mrs Lana Norman
(017687) 70204
Cragg Farm
Buttermere
Cockermouth
CUMBRIA CA13 9XA

Buttermere - continued

Mrs & Mrs Parker
(017687) 70233
Dalegarth
Buttermere
Nr Cockermouth CA13 9XA

YOUTH HOSTELS

The hostels listed below are located on or near the trails. See opposite for telephone numbers and grid references.
Keswick
Borrowdale
Derwentwater
Buttermere
Honister Hause

CAMPING BARNS

The following barns are located near to the trails:
Eagle's Nest
Cat Bells
Cragg

See Camping Barns column on this page for exact locations and booking details.

CAMPING

Derwentwater, Keswick
Tel (017687) 72392

Castlerigg Hall, Keswick
Tel (017687) 72479

Hollows Farm, Grange
Tel (017687) 77298

Chapel House Farm, Grange
Tel (017687) 77602

Ashness Farm, Ashness
Tel (017687) 77361

Sykes Farm, Buttermere
Tel (017687) 70222

Dalegarth Farm, Buttermere
Tel (017687) 70233

To & through Cumbria and the Lake District

Cumbria County Council publishes this excellent map and travel guide to the Lake District - available from Tourist Information Centres.

Journey Planner

The **Journey Planner** service is also operated by Cumbria County Council

Tel: (01228) 606000
Mon - Fri 0900-1700
Sat 0900-1200

Internet
http://www.wwwebguides.com/pubtrans/cumbria/info.html.

Buses

Stagecoach Cumberland operate bus services throughout the Lake District. Their **Lakeland Explorer Summer Timetable** contains timetables for all buses in the area. Available free from the Tourist Information Centres listed on page 80 or write to:

Stagecoach Cumberland
PO Box 17
Tangier Street
Whitehaven
Cumbria CA28 7XF

A telephone Bus Information service is also available Monday to Saturday 7am - 7pm and Sunday 9am - 5.30pm.
Tel: (01946) 63222

The National Trust
Operate free summer Sunday services to Tarn Howes and to Watendlath.
Tel: (015393) 35599

Boats

Timetable Information is available on the following numbers :

Lake Windermere
Tel: (015395) 31188

Coniston Water
Tel: (015394) 36216

Ullswater
Tel: (01539) 721626

Derwent Water
Tel: (017687) 72263

Trains

The Lakes and Furness Line
This serves Oxenholme, Kendal, Burnside, Staveley, and Windermere and Carnforth, Silverdale, Arnside, Grange-over-Sands, Kents Bank, Cark, Ulverston, Dalton, Roose and Barrow. Through trains are available from Liverpool, Manchester, Preston and Lancaster

The Cumbrian Coast Line
This operates between Carlisle and Barrow serving Wigton, Aspatria, Maryport, Workington, Whitehaven, St Bees, Sellafield, Ravenglass, Millom and Askham.

Tel : 0800 156158 for free copies of timetables and line guides.

Ravenglass and Eskdale narrow gauge railway

Train Enquiries (01229) 717171

The Lakeside & Haverthwaite steam railway

Train Enquiries (015395) 31594

Heritage Trail Transport

The bus services below operated in 1997 between 23rd March and 1st November. The departure times are for guidance only and current timetables should be obtained from Tourist Information Centres.

The Borrowdale Bus to and from Grange allows the Lakeland Heritage Trail route to to be completed as three separate short linear walks.

The Buttermere Bus from Buttermere provides the option of returning to Keswick at the end of the first day of the Mountain Trail and travelling back the next day to rejoin the walk.

The Borrowdale Bus No 79

Keswick bus station - Grange
Departures at 0925, 1025, 1125, 1225, 1425, 1525, 1625, 1740
Grange - Keswick
Departures at 1005, 1105, 1205, 1305, 1505, 1605, 1705, 1820
Journey time approx 20 minutes

The Buttermere Bus No 77 & 77A

Keswick bus station - Buttermere
Departures at 1025 and 1425 via Whinlatter and 0840 and 1605 via Seatoller
Buttermere - Keswick
Departures at 1110 and 1510 via Seatoller and 0932 and 1657 via Whinlatter
Journey time approx 40 minutes

The Keswick Launch

Clockwise and anti-clockwise services operate round Derwent Water from Keswick calling at Ashness Gate, Lodore, High Brandelhow, Low Brandelhow, Hawes End, Nichol End - departures hourly.

Ramblers' Association

Going for a walk gives everyone a unique sense of freedom. Whether you are on a demanding track on the fells or just taking the dog for a stroll you are enjoying a recreation chosen by a quarter of the population.
The possibility of wandering freely over open uncultivated ground is regarded as a natural right in many countries. But what most of us do not realise is that it has taken over 60 years of dedicated lobbying by one highly effective pressure group to achieve what we now enjoy: a national footpath network, national parks like the Lake District and access to thousands of acres of open land. We take them for granted but without the persistent efforts of The Ramblers working at parliamentary and local levels, they would not exist at all. Fifteen million of us enjoy walking. The protective muscle of The Ramblers is sustained by a growing supporter base of over 190,000 people of all ages. Local groups have been instrumental in the creation of a number of trails including the Allerdale Ramble and the Cumbria Way.
Members receive copies of the quarterly colour magazine Rambling Today and the Rambler's Yearbook & Accommodation Guide.
For further information and details of the current subscription rates send SAE to:
The Ramblers' Association
1/5 Wandsworth Road,
London SW8 2XX

Long Distance Walkers Association

The LDWA was founded in 1972 and although it caters for all types of long distance walker its primary interest is in organised challenge events.
It now has a dedicated following of some seven thousand members with local groups in all parts of the country. One of the main attractions of membership is the receipt of their magazine appropriately called **Strider.** This has regular news on published long distance routes of all types, news of local group activities, general articles plus a comprehensive calendar of organised challenge events.
Sponsored walks and charity walks fall outside the scope of the LDWA along with race walking and racing.
Send SAE with enquiries to:
Membership Secretary,
10 Temple Park Close, Leeds,
West Yorks LS15 OJJ

Lakeland Challenge Events

These are walks which are organised annually on specific dates each year and have to be entered in advance. They should not be confused with charity walks. In most cases walkers are given a brief route description linking a number of checkpoints through which they have to pass. For organisational reasons a time limit is imposed; certificates and badges are awarded for successful completions. The Lakes Four Three - thousands organised by the Ramblers' Association is probably the best known while local goups of the LDWA often organise low key events in some of the less frequented areas of the Lakes. The LDWA's Strider magazine is the best source of information on these walks .

Fell Runners

The FRA was founded in 1970 to encourage and foster better standards of fell running and mountain racing throughout the United Kingdom.
Membership benefits include three magazines per year and an annual fixtures calendar and handbook listing over 200 races. The magazine incudes regular news on long distance runs and peak bagging rounds.

SAE with enquiries to:
Membership Secretary,
34a Kirkland, Kendal, Cumbria
LA9 5AD

Conservation

The ravages of nature, the Lakeland weather and the pounding of thousands of boots are taking their toll on the fragile landscape of the Lake District. The National Park authority and the National Trust are working in partnership with others to repair the damage and ensure access and safety. But this work is very costly. The Lake District Tourism and Conservation Partnership is appealing for support for essential work to continue. Just one metre of footpath costs £15.00 to repair. Help secure the future of the Lakes by sending donations payable to *Invest in the Lakes* to:

Lake District Tourism and Conservation Partnership,
Brockhole Visitor Centre,
Windermere,
Cumbria LA23 1LJ

Please play your part in conserving the Lakeland landscape.

The National Park

The Lake Distict is the largest of Britain's national parks established in the 1950's. Within its 885 square miles is a blend of mountains and lakes that represent some of Europe's finest landscape. The National Park is managed by The National Park Authority which is funded by public money. They regulate development, look after the landscape and help visitors to appreciate the special qualities of the National Park. In looking after the landscape they work in partnership with other organisations such as the National Trust to ensure sensitive land management and access to 1800 miles of footpaths. Their Rangers and Voluntary Wardens carry out wide-ranging conservation work. A network of information centres, publications, educational courses and an extensive events programme have been developed to cater for some 14 million visitors each year.

Charity Walks

Sponsored walks in the countryside are a popular means by which money is raised for charities. None of the routes in this book are recommended for large scale sponsored walks. An influx of a large number of people into an area could prove to be intrusive and disruptive for both locals and other holidaymakers as well as damaging to footpaths and the general environment. The Lake District is a particularly fragile and sensitive area and already suffers from erosion problems. The organisation of large groups or events requires careful management and consultation. The National Park Authority will be pleased to assist and advise. They can be contacted at Murley Moss, Oxenholme Road, Kendal, Cumria LA9 7RL
Tel: (01539) 724555

WEATHERLINE SERVICE

017687 - 75757

Use The National Park's 24 Hour Line before you leave for your walk

local weather updated twice daily

Food

There are no miracle foods which make a long day on the hills feel like an afternoon stroll! Practice, inherent ability and long-term bodily adjustment are more important factors in performance.
A general rule for eating during long walks is little and often so that the body does not become overloaded with the burden of digestion as well as muscular activity.
Generally the body is the best guide to immediate food and drink requirements. As muscle activity and sweat loss deplete the body of vital substances, preferences for types of food change. Foods which are readily attractive, palatable and digestible under normal conditions can differ from those required when fatigue is beginning to set in. Discovering which foods do or do not suit you is largely a matter of trial and error.
Sweet foods such as glucose are usually consumed to assist energy output. The rule of little and often applies here otherwise the body may over-react producing a low blood sugar level which may leave you feeling even more fatigued.

Safety and Equipment

Most of the walks described in this book require a sound knowledge of map reading, equipment and safety. Most published guides include relevant advice; here is a reminder of some important points.

☐ Unless you are confident of your experience and ability under all conditions go with a group. Statistics show more injuries to lone walkers than those in groups.

☐ Be prepared for sudden changes in the weather. Friendly, inviting sunny weather can quickly transform into wet, misty conditions particularly on higher fells.

☐ Devise a route schedule allowing plenty of time before nightfall and monitor your progress against it.

☐ Do not be reluctant to abandon your planned route in the event of deteriorating weather conditions.

☐ Leave word of your route or put a note in your car.

☐ Obtain a local weather forecast before setting out.

☐ Note the position of telephone boxes and possible escape routes.

☐ The distress signal is six whistle blows or torch flashes, pause a minute and then repeat.

☐ Check you have the following :
•Map and map case
•compass and whistle
•waterproof jacket and trousers
•woollen hat and gloves
•Drink and food to eat en-route
•spare jumper and socks
•Emergency rations
•Survival bag
•Torch and first-aid kit
•Tenpence pieces for phone
•Boots with patterned sole
•Walk schedule and pencil

Christian Aid
We believe in life before death

To bring about real, lasting change in the lives of the poorest people we must tackle the roots of poverty. This is where our campaigning and educational work comes in - to change attitudes about poverty, and to change the structures that cause poverty. Here are some examples of our work.

ACTION ... Our Who Runs the World campaign highlighted how World Bank and International Monetary Fund policies damaged schools, hospitals, jobs and the environment in the developing world. The more recent Great Supermarket Receipt Collection is urging supermarkets to ensure workers from the developing world who produce their goods receive basic rights, such as a minimum wage and safety at work. The UK's top ten supermarkets make more money in a year than the world's 35 poorest countries combined. To celebrate the Millennium we are looking for your help to create the biggest petition in the history of the world - The Jubilee 2000 Petition - to cancel the unpayable debts owed by the world's poorest countries.

PRESSURE ... We have also published reports highlighting the discrepancies between rich and poor. We have tackled sports companies who pay a pittance to Asian workers making sports shoes and footballs , yet charge extortionate prices for them in the shops.

EDUCATION ... We have worked hard to enable children in the UK and Ireland and children overseas to come closer - to see how much they have in common. Over 300,000 children read *Global Gang,* our children's newspaper, and 20,000 young people attended Greenbelt, the annual Christian music and arts festival supported by Christian Aid.

Christian Aid is an agency of the British and Irish churches working with the world's poor in over 60 countries. It is part of ACT International (Action by Churches Together), the world-wide ecumenical network for emergency relief.

" We will strengthen our support for the world's poorest communities as they struggle for life and for justice"

Who promotes the campaigns, raises the funds and spreads the word? It could not be done without a nationwide network of volunteers, individuals, young and old, of many faiths and of none, from as far apart as Penzance and Perth.

For information on current campaigns or to make a donation write to:

Christian Aid
PO Box 100
LONDON SE1 7RT

Registered Charity Number 258003

Amnesty International UK

What does Amnesty do?

Like many organisations, Amnesty has a mandate which limits and defines our work. That mandate has four main parts which are based directly on the United Nations' Universal Declaration of Human Rights of 1948. The organisation actively campaigns to:

- Free all Prisoners of Conscience. These are people detained anywhere for their beliefs or because of their ethnic origin, sex, colour or language - who have not used or advocated violence.
- Ensure fair and prompt trials for political prisoners.
- Abolish the death penalty, torture, and other cruel treatment of prisoners.
- End extrajudicial executions and "disappearances".

Since 1961 Amnesty International has principally campaigned on behalf of Prisoners of Conscience. Recently the movement has responded to new patterns in human rights violations around the world and has taken action on behalf of victims of many other forms of abuse. Increasingly the organisation devotes its resources to:

- Working against abuses by opposition groups including hostage taking, torture and killings of prisoners and other arbitrary killings.
- Campaigning for asylum seekers who are at risk of being returned to a country where they might be held as Prisoners of Conscience, "disappear" , or suffer torture or execution.
- Helping people who, because of the non-violent expression of their beliefs, or by reason of their ethnic origin, sex, colour, or language, are forcibly exiled from their country.

" It is better to light a candle than curse the darkness "

Few people are aware of their ability to effect change in the world. Commitment from people like you from all five continents and every walk of life helps Amnesty to campaign effectively against human rights violations. The thousands of closed case files are testament to the power of the individual. The more members we have the louder our voice.

To become a member or make a donation write to;

Amnesty International UK
99-119 Roseberry Avenue
LONDON EC1R 4RE

Nobel Peace Prize 1977
UN Human Rights Prize 1978

INDEX OF TRAILS

Allerdale Ramble 27
Alternative Coast to Coast 65
Ancient Ways of Lakeland 61

Back O' Skidda 28
Bob Graham Round 68
Borrowdale Round 76
Buttermere Round 76

Charnley Way 29
Cistercian Way 30
Coledale Round 78
Cumberland Way 31
Cumbria Coastal Way 32
Cumbria Way 33
Cumbrian Classic Trident Walk 61

Dales Way 66
Duddon Horseshoe 34
Duddon Landscape 35
Duddon Triangle 36

Ennerdale Horseshoe 77
Everest Challenge 37

Fairfield Horseshoe 77
Footpath Touring 61
Four Passes Walk 63
Furness Boundary Walk 38
Furness Five Trigs 39
Furness Trail 61
Furness Way 40

Grasmere Skyline Classic 41

Haematite Trail 42
High Street Stroll 47

In Search Of Westmorland 62

John Merrill's Lakeland Challenge 62
Joss Naylor's Lakeland Challenge 75

Kentmere Round 77
Kirkbymoor Round 48

Lake District Boundary Walk 49
Lakeland Fringe 61
Lakeland Heritage Trail 10
Lakeland Heritage Mountain Trail 18
Lakeland Ridges Challenge 50
Lakeland Round 51
Lakeland to Lindisfarne 65
Lakeland Top Ten 61
Lakeland's Ten Highest Peaks 75
Lakes and Meres 75
Lakes Link 61
Lakes Four Three-thousands 74
Lakes Three Old County Summits 74
Lakes 2500's 75
Lancashire to Lakeland 66
Lancaster Canal 66
Langdale Circuit 78
Leeds Town Hall to Scafell Pike 75
Limestone Link 66
Lost Lancs Way 63

Mosedale Horseshoe 78

Newlands Round 78
North of England Way 65

Pennington Round 62

Ravenber 65
Rydal Round 52

Shap to Ravenglass 75
Shap Stroll 62

That's Lyth 63
Thirlmere Round 53
Thirlmere Way 66
Traditional Hostels Lakes Walk 54

Ullswater Circuit 63

Wainwright's Coast to Coast 65
Wainwright's Lakeland Tour 55
Walk Round The Lakes 56
Walking Through the Lake District 62
Walking Tour of Lakeland 62
Wasdale Circuit 78
West Lakes Way 57
Westmorland Heritage Walk 58
Westmorland Way 59
Whicham Valley Five Trigs 60

Castlerigg Stone Circle, Keswick